WILLIAM L. F

AN EXPERIMENT
IN MINDFULNESS

AN EXPERIMENT
IN MINDFULNESS

An English Admiral's Experiences
in a Buddhist Monastery

E. H. SHATTOCK

1960

E. P. DUTTON & CO., INC.

New York

First published in the U.S.A., 1960
By E. P. Dutton & Co., Inc.

FIRST EDITION

3/96

Library of Congress Catalog Card Number: 60-6073

Gift.

CONTENTS

1   THE BEGINNING   7

2   SETTLING IN   20

3   FIRST STEPS   33

4   THE MIND AT BAY   46

5   THE SATIPATTHANA METHOD   61

6   NO SOUL, NO GOD   72

7   SOME THOUGHTS ON MIND   87

8   ON DIMENSIONS AND TIME   101

9   DISTRACTIONS   121

10 AFTERMATH   139

AN EXPERIMENT
IN MINDFULNESS

I

THE BEGINNING

A GOOD many books have appeared recently on the subject
of meditation. Some of these have been excellent and have
treated the subject as one with which the ordinary average
person could concern himself without being considered a
crank. Others have been very technical and somewhat
bewildering, and have left the reader with the impression
that only a superman could carry out the routine and pro-
cedures that were required. It is not my purpose to add to
these books of instruction, but to relate my own experience
in undergoing a special course of meditation in the Thathana
Yeiktha at Rangoon. I think this may be of interest to
others, not because of any particular aptitude for meditation or of any special knowledge I may have, but for the
very reverse. Possessing no particular psychic qualities
or leanings towards mysticism, and being of certainly no
more than the average spiritual stature, the degree to which
I was able to take this course of Satipatthana in my stride,
my experiences during the process of coming to grips with
my mind, and the results, were what any other person

7

temporarily abandoning their daily occupation could expect.

During the course, as will be explained later, I had to change my habits of eating and sleeping drastically, and my daily routine might seem too severe to be undertaken voluntarily. But, in fact, my Western habits dropped from me without effort or discomfort, probably because I was living at a much reduced tempo. And, of course, I was among so many others all doing the same thing, like a boy at a new school who slips into the routine without realizing that it is in parts extremely tiresome!

In Burma it is quite common for laymen to attend for this particular course, and once or twice during their business life, and certainly again on retiring, many Burmese men, some of them prominent in the affairs of their country, go to one of the meditation centres for a period of strict meditation practice of usually not less than six weeks. During my time, among many others, the chief of Rangoon police, who had just retired, was there for a 'refresher' course: he came to see me one day and explained why he felt the necessity of doing this. In the cell next to mine was a young man who was the owner of a chain of sterilized milk factories rapidly spreading throughout Rangoon. He appeared to be a very active and worldly young man, and he had already done one period at the Thathana. In his case I don't think he was taking it as seriously as the others, for his wife came to see him every day, and he was inclined to be sociable with the other 'students'.

Although there was no supervision of the daily routine, both talking and reading were strongly discouraged. This was particularly so for those doing the course of strict meditation; for the monks, many of whom were there for much longer periods, these activities were rigidly curtailed.

It may be wondered what decided me to try my hand at meditation, and why I should choose to do it in a Buddhist monastery. Both these are very pertinent questions, and since the justification of this book depends on the answers to them having a significance for other people, I would like to digress somewhat from the main story of the book in order to make it clear from the outset what was the spur and what the reason for an action that many of my friends have considered, at the least, unusual.

Few of us would willingly exchange our present existence for one of, say, two hundred years ago, unless we could be guaranteed that the exchange would land us among the leisured class. And even then, in spite of the romance that at this safe distance colours much of the ordinary living of those days, as shewn in films and portrayed in many novels, we should find the rugged, coarse, and often insanitary life little to our liking. Stripped of this false romance, the ills and discomforts of those years stand out in sharp perspective when examined with the happier experience of our present-day life; and we are now so tuned to comfort and convenience that it would be a disillusioning shock if we found ourselves permanently set in an environment where they were absent.

It is precisely this sort of impression that someone two hundred years from now would have about the conditions in which we live today; but it is difficult when living in the middle of them to detect the things that are harming us. We get used to them and accept them, and in many cases do not even realize that they are harmful. If in fact some people do observe the habits and customs of our civilization that are hurtful, there is little they can do about it. The surge of progress brings these evils with it, and they are carried along protected by the advantages with which they are associated. But quite a little can be done by the individual to lessen the impact of the destructive forces that are building up around us, provided we know that they exist and can recognize them; and it is with the outlook of the individual towards the things that are tending to stifle his power to remain on top of events that this book is mainly concerned. It requires a new understanding of the source of that power, coupled with the knowledge of the technique of developing it. But it is difficult to raise much enthusiasm in ourselves for any drastic reorientation of our outlook, for on the whole we are too satisfied with the improvements we have made to living to notice what is going on, and we are not tempted to look at today with the eyes of the future.

Many of the changes that hygiene and devices for our comfort have brought in the past hundred and fifty years have not all been advantageous. We have vastly increased the proportion of our population that reach old age without being able to provide them with more than bare existence. We have eradicated many diseases that were a scourge and decimator of populations, and incidentally introduced new and more perplexing ones. We have tremendously lessened human suffering and increased the entertainment of the masses, without being able to make it constructive. We are, in fact, better produced, better kept and protected, and far better educated (if we know what that means) than our forbears of two hundred years ago. But we are in danger of becoming over-protected against the things that the body can resist of itself, though not, of course, to the satisfaction of the idealists; and we are laying ourselves open to a host of insidious and far more complex abnormalities. We are living on sterilization, immunization, and prophylaxis; and these measures will go on continuing until we are pumped full of every kind of preventive, including those to prevent the bugs getting used to the remedies on which we are relying. And there will be less and less cause for the body to build any defences of its own.

The physical aspect of too much protection is certainly not the worst that the so-called improvements in living conditions have done to us. The never-ceasing racket of modern life penetrates every fibre of our being during our waking hours, and often during sleep. The rapid succession of events, private, national, and international, and before long interplanetary as well, keeps us jumping from emotion to emotion, from tension to tension, and our adrenal glands working overtime. If there is a pause in this feverish tickling of our hackles, we are bored. We have become accustomed to the unceasing stimulation of our senses and do not know how to occupy our minds when it is absent. This symptom too is being taken care of by drugs. There are drugs to relax us and drugs to zip us up when we have finished our relaxation. There are drugs to send us to sleep and others to help us keep awake. The same thing is happening to relieve the mind of much of its natural task as is happening in the case of the body, but with far more serious and far-reaching consequences; its defences are being undermined; the power that it holds within itself is not being given a chance to develop a natural antidote. The need for an inborn antidote to the increased nerve strain to which we are now normally subjected is of the very greatest importance. But as yet there is none.

'But look,' somebody may say, 'how easy it is for everybody to enjoy some sort of relaxation; and with the shorter working hours that automation will bring, there will be even greater opportunities.' This, however, is a prospect that threatens an even greater incidence of diseases derived from nervous tension, unless the danger is seen in time and steps are taken to prepare the people for living with leisure. For relaxation in many cases only means introducing a different set of tensions, and real relaxation is almost unknown. This may sound an exaggerated and pessimistic picture of what is after all a reasonably pleasant existence; and perhaps it is. But it is true that we have largely lost the art of relaxing, and what is replacing, or in many cases has irretrievably replaced, the quieter pursuits of olden days, neither requires us to participate, nor soothes us. We are becoming watchers of the few, and the few are becoming adept at providing what we think we want. It is watching and at the same time identifying ourselves with one or other of the performers that does the harm. At the cinema we feel the joys and agonies of the hero or heroine as though they were ours. At the football match it is our foot that kicks the goal or misses it. And once again our emotions are bursting their bounds and our adrenal glands hastening to deal with all these emergencies as though they were our own. To anyone who stops to think where this sort of life is leading, there comes a longing to stop the racket for a moment, to savour the refreshing power of stillness and peace; to bring the immense quiet of the mountains into one's Chelsea bedsitting room, and to carry the joy that the smell of a spring meadow brings into the chores of one's daily life. It is comparatively easy to jump into an aeroplane and fly to the mountains or lakes of Switzerland, but it is becoming increasingly difficult to recapture the feeling, too impersonal, wide, and embracing to be called an emotion, that fills our minds when we are face to face with the superb dignity of nature. The aeroplane trip is no substitute for this: at best it is a temporary alleviation of the process of disintegration; but unfortunately we think it is so. In truth the mind does not need mountains or seas to stir its depths or to reveal its grandeur. But we are forgetting this, and if we do not encourage the habit of developing the mind's power of rehabilitating itself, we shall lose the sense of our own uniqueness, and become an insignificant portion of the mass mind.

We need to do two things: to cultivate this feeling of abstracting ourselves from an outside world into an inner seclusion where security is self-generating and strength is in acquiescence rather than in activity; and to develop a permanent insulation from the shocks and tensions of modern life.

These thoughts had been gradually taking form during what was mostly an energetic and active life. It was a life, however, that had many opportunities for quiet thought— as officer of the watch on the bridge of a ship at night, away off the traffic routes with no troubles to disturb the long hours, and only the swish and rippling of the water along the ship's sides as a whispered background to one's thinking. And sometimes, too, in the air with a healthy-sounding engine bringing me back from an exercise over the sea, I became convinced that an antidote to the tension-producing novelties that surround us must be planned and consciously developed; and it must be employed regularly.

Why not religion?

Such an obvious question! And one that demands a convincing answer. A simple and honest one would be that religion as I interpret, express, and experience it, is not it. But this is merely an individual expression which in itself may be no more than an admission of failure. But the failure is so general that it must be one on both sides. To many, the simple fact of what is wrong with Christianity is that it just hasn't grown up with the requirements of the people. It is still talking in childish terms: much of its dogma is unacceptable, and much unintelligible. There is far too much of the man-made and too little of the Christ-made about it; and what men have added has been used to extend the childish allegories, or in complication of simplicities. It isn't even up to date on its own admission: some of the exhortations still contained in the prayer-book read like echoes of the medieval torture chambers. I do not deny that to many it brings comfort. It is a comfort won by transferring the burden, and taking what others think without using that thoroughly healthy, critical faculty that is our birthright as human beings. Is this what I really think? Is this my experience, or am I borrowing from others and being too lazy or too timid to discover whether their thoughts and beliefs can truly become mine by the certitude of experience? Religious prayer as the antidote is too formal, and even when not formalized by habit is too anthropomorphic, to use an ugly but expressive word. The technique of prayer as taught is immature. The adult Christian mind must be able to see further than God as a Father, or as an infinitely wise Judge, and Christ as His Son. These are childish allegories that no longer satisfy, except the few.

No, not religion. It is too complicated, and I felt I needed something less contaminated than Christianity had become: something preferably with as few labels as possible. There would be nothing to prevent this new source leading to a deeper and more fruitful practice of one's religion, whatever it might be, but it should be a source that was, as far as any could be, free from religious thought itself. I was anxious, too, to avoid anything that employed emotion as a vehicle or even as an element in the process of acquiring the ability to capture moments of serenity; for the world is already suffering from a surfeit of emotion everywhere, and it can be a most unreliable, misleading, and dangerous guide. Besides which, I would like my solution to be applicable to everyone, and for this to be so it would be better to keep clear of anything that involved particular religious beliefs. It is emotion that has divided Christianity into a multitude of factions, and that led to the shameful spectacle of history's religious wars. Emotion is the slayer of tolerance. I would myself become involved in its intemperate convictions if I could not learn how to go beyond it.

Meditation was obviously a possible way of tapping the source I was looking for. But it was to me a somewhat nebulous undertaking associated either with Yoga or religious devotion. The word itself has a fearsome meaning to some, and conjures up something that only the spiritual and saintly can indulge in. That is, of course, a quite erroneous impression: the most unspiritual of us indulge in meditation of a sort every day, but almost unaware and certainly uncontrolled. Whenever we think about something to the exclusion of everything else we are meditating. Prayer is sometimes meditation, though the mere repetition of set phrases is not. Deep contemplation of religious subjects is meditation of a particular kind that is tinged with emotional overtones. The Eastern religions and systems of spiritual development, in particular Buddhism and Yoga, have a wealth of experience of the various stages of meditation that can be reached by the man who is going about his daily work, and of the deeper stages that can be entered, step by step, where eventually the intellectual or mental content vanishes. It seemed to me that here was something worth looking into, because it eliminated emotion and did not necessitate a religious setting.

The first thing that confronts anyone who studies any of the systems of meditation that abound in the East is that a degree of mind control far above anything that the average Westerner possesses is necessary. This fact is a most discouraging one if he starts practising any of the simpler exercises, and it is probable that he gives up in despair with the conviction that our minds are different to the Eastern mind which is born to patience and passivity, and has endless time in which to make use of these qualities. But this revelation of a 'butterfly' mind should be a challenge to us who pride ourselves on our achievements in all branches of theoretical and practical science. In our minds we have the most miraculous and powerful tool that the human being possesses, but we do not bother to see that we get the most out of it. Few of us know how to employ it efficiently, and probably use no more that ten per cent of its real capacity. We take care to stuff our minds with all sorts of information, much of which has to be corrected at regular intervals, but we take no pains to learn how to develop the full power and efficiency of this wonderful machine. No industrialist would accept in the machines of his factory the waste of energy that goes on in our minds, the inefficient methods with which we employ them, and the lack of proper rest we allow them. When a machine is not working it is resting, and the friction of its moving parts is no longer wearing the machine out; nor is it any longer using up electric power, oil, or water. But we have not learnt how to put our minds into this state except by accident, or when we are in deep sleep and not dreaming. The ability to relax the mind consciously is of very great value. True meditation is relaxation, and the deeper and more 'formless' it is, the greater is the recuperative effect on the whole human system. Meditation, therefore, is a really practical occupation: it is in no sense necessarily a religious one, though it is usually thought of as such. It is itself basically academic, practical, and profitable. It is, I think, necessary to emphasize this point, because so many only associate meditation with holy or saintly people, and regard it as an advanced form of the pious life.

During my life I had tried other methods of 'getting away from things' and letting the peace of an existence temporarily, without compulsion, soak into my being and counteract the stresses set up by the pace and anxieties of normal living, but I found that although I benefited in each case, the echo soon faded, and I could not carry back into my daily life anything more active than a memory. This was not enough, but it at least kept the realization alive that there was much to be gained from learning how to live more as a detached watcher of the busy scene and less as an unwilling participator. Without pursuing the subject with any sense of urgency, I gradually grew to feel that if I could find a method of meditation that was free from emotional and religious complications, and could reasonably be fitted into a normal daily routine, it would be what I needed. And not only I, but everyone who felt that their proper nature was being cramped and distorted by the continuous and almost unperceived tensions of modern life.

By chance, I came across a book which described what seemed to me to be just such a method, and I studied it carefully to see whether it was something which I thought I could undertake. It was a fairly detailed account by a Ceylon Buddhist who had taken a course in Satipatthana at a training centre in Rangoon. Satipatthana is a method of mind training initiated by the Buddha and reintroduced into Burma by a Buddhist priest, Mahasi Sayadaw, who runs the Centre at Rangoon, where this training is given to priests and laymen. It was simple, so simple in fact that its very simplicity turned out to be one of its main difficulties! And it required no philosophical understanding, nor any particular religious beliefs. I did not think it would be possible to derive much benefit from any sort of meditation unless one started off with a concentrated period of practice under conditions that were at least helpful. It was difficult to find such conditions in the sort of life I was leading. But it so happened that an opportunity presented itself of my going to Rangoon where this monk had done his course, so I wrote to the Buddhist Council to ask whether it would be possible for me to undertake the training. I had a most encouraging reply and a very generous offer to defray my living expenses during my time there. I accordingly made plans to spend four weeks' leave doing the course on the conclusion of my present duty, and accepted the fact that it would be generally supposed that I was about to become a Buddhist. But it will be clear, now, that this is not the tale of a conversion, but of an attempt to test the re-action of a well-tried Eastern system on a typical Western mind.

2

SETTLING IN

IT WAS a simple journey to Rangoon by air, requiring only a change and a fairly long stop at Bangkok. The question of what clothes to take had given me some thought as I had been warned that it would be very hot in Rangoon in February and March, and I had little idea what the living conditions in the Centre would be. In a tropical climate one has to change several times a day, and either have a very efficient laundry service at one's beck and call, or an ample supply of cotton shirts, etc., which would have made my luggage rather bulky, and I particularly did not want to arrive looking like a European tourist. In the end I decided to take a few cotton sarongs and shirts, and bank on being able to do what laundry was necessary myself. As it turned out, the Buddhist Council presented me with two longyis, which are the Burmese equivalent of the sarong, and one of the helpers at the Centre did my laundry for a very small sum.

On arrival at Bangkok I found the airport packed with thousands of spectators who had come to watch a display of mainly American air power. Some hundred odd large American troop carriers were parked round the airfield, and later these took off and dropped thousands of paratroopers accurately in the centre of the field. Jet fighters screamed over the enthralled crowds, who were, I think, more delighted at the picturesque scene of the many coloured parachutes floating gracefully down from a deep blue sky than impressed by what it all signified. It was the sort of sky that made such a superb background for the golden pinnacles and domes of the temples that could be seen everywhere. This display of military might seemed so out of place in a country where peace was understood as a driving attitude of mind and not as preventive armaments. It was difficult to see how these people could regard S.E.A.T.O., under whose auspices the show was being put on, as a harbinger of security for their country. Buddhism has always been such a non-militant religion, and the fact that new ideologies existed that regarded all means of forcing their beliefs on the not yet enlightened as justifiable is one that will not quickly change an outlook that is the habit of centuries.

The smooth running of this large and important airfield was badly disorganized during the time of the display, and my K.L.M. connection to Rangoon was delayed. Such delays, which occur so frequently when travelling by air, are usually exasperating and tedious, but this one was enlivened by the spectacle of thousands of Thailanders, who had come by car and train and on foot from Bangkok, all in their brightest clothes, making a kaleidoscope of colour and gaiety that had little connection with the ominous portents of the demonstration itself. There were, of course, a great number of children, the little girls always serious and dignified, and the boys scampering around enjoying the freedom of a new playground. Everywhere family groups were sitting quietly on seats or on the ground outside, waiting patiently for the next burst of colour in the sky. They were not eating, as would have been the case in almost any Western country, but some were drinking highly coloured juices out of glasses that were afterwards hurriedly washed in a pail of water that would have to last the whole day. Outside in the road I had seen the little push or tricycle carts that sell cooked rice and hot soups doing a roaring trade. There, too, though it was long after the start of the display, motor-tricycle rickshaws were continually arriving with their gaily-coloured cargoes sitting incongruously in these horrible products of Western civilization. There was none of these in Singapore, and I was to see none in Burma; only in Thailand had these noisy and smelly replacements of the rickshaw runner caught on. Of course they could travel to distances outside the town, such as this, which would be beyond the capabilities of a runner, but the dust and noise they kicked up played hell with the peaceful countryside. So did the buses. They were an infliction that could only have been endured by a people born to patient acceptance of a hard lot. They were strange miniature erections on what was probably a small car chassis, and designed for a maximum number of seats with a minimum of comfort. They dashed along with a rattle and abandon that triumphantly disregarded what must have been their imminent disintegration. In a few cases this had already overtaken them, and their passengers, quite undaunted, piled into others, also full to bursting, that happened to pass at that moment. They were off again, bright scarves fluttering from the windows and the young people leaning out to bandy remarks with the overtaking and the overtaken. For although the traffic was in a solid line as far as could be seen from the airfield, the overtaking game was being played in earnest, and with frantic hooting cars and buses would haul out and gesticulate themselves into the line farther up, the drivers letting go the wheel entirely to show exactly where they were going to cut in, and why. It was an exciting scene, and the sweating bus loads seemed to accept it all as part of the entertainment.

The call for my flight came through, and in a very short time I was off. The activity of the crowd, a moment ago so personal and intimate, receded into stillness, and what had been groups of eager and excited people became patches of an indiscriminate brown-grey with an occasional flash as the sun caught some glass or jewelled ornament. It was a disillusioning feeling, the depersonalizing effect of the 'view from above'. I had often felt this when flying as a pilot, but in an airliner it was an impression that was usually fleeting and almost unnoticed, as one's attention was busy with the immediate business of settling down to the luxury of having nothing to do but sleep, eat, and read, until the next stop. But as I now looked down on the amorphous mass of human beings whose outline was merging with the roofs and trees, and with the whole busy picture rapidly slipping into the indistinct distance, I tried to imagine myself both here with a god's view of the insignificance of mankind and at the same time down there taking part in their joys and discomforts. It was almost a parallel to the sort of solution I was looking for, except that my two impressions existed one after the other in a time sequence. If it was to be possible to avoid the corrosive effect of too much and too strong emotion, the sequence must be eliminated. The view must be simultaneously from the inside and from above, and too impersonal and callous an outlook be prevented by a knowledge of the intimacy of joy and suffering.

It was just getting dark when we arrived at Rangoon, that short period between sunset and night that always seemed to me to demonstrate that in the tropics the sun was the only thing that was hurrying. I strolled with the other passengers to a rather woebegone hut that held the temporary offices until the airport buildings were completed. There were apparently many formalities to be gone through and I waited a little bewildered, seeing no notices in any language I could understand and hearing no English. I had not been there long, however, before two representatives of the Buddhist Council had picked me out and come to my rescue. It could not have been difficult for them; I was about the only one in European dress, all the remainder were wearing longyis and shirts, and most had added a jacket, for the evenings at this time were still cool. I was quickly cleared and whisked away in a car to Rangoon where I was entertained to supper before being taken to the Meditation Centre.

The term Meditation Centre is the proper translation of the Burmese words *Thathana Yeiktha* (pronounced with long a's and in *Thathana* the accent is on the first 'tha'.), and although it is mainly occupied by monks, most but not all of whom are doing the Satipatthana training, accommodation is also available for laymen in the various blocks of cells. In Western terms it is a staff college for mind training, and, with its austere living routine and long hours of work, a pretty tough one. There are no religious ceremonies that the laymen are obliged to attend, but they are expected to 'take' and live by the five moral precepts accepted by all

monks, and which I shall refer to later. These would remain
in force during the period of the training. The few administrative monks and some doing instructional work or looking
after shrines in the neighbourhood had all presumably done
the course, for it is through this training that they obtain
insight and learn the truths of the Buddhist doctrine by
first-hand experience. This can only be done after they have
learnt to control and still the mind.

I had imagined that I was going to stay at a monastery,
and visualized a large, imposing building in a remote part of
Burma, situated on the side of a mountain, or at least on
top of a hill, romantic, inaccessible, aloof, the sort of thing
one had often seen in pictures. But it was none of these
things. The Centre lay just off the main road, almost on
the outskirts of Rangoon, about five miles from the middle
of the town, and not in the least isolated, either physically
from the surrounding houses, or from the noise and bustle
of the main road that carried the traffic between Rangoon
and the airport. As we drove through the gate, I noticed
on each side a gilded papier-mâché dragon that had presumably added to the gaiety of some festival, but now looked
tawdry and uncared-for, and somewhat out of place. That
the fervour of some important celebration should now be
represented by these sorry relics is a thought that I find
taints all ruins, the tattered remnants of man's once living
ideals and aspirations that could not stand the strain of
being kept alive. There seemed to be no plan or order in
the arrangement of the buildings, and I was aware of a
scattered haphazard collection of huts, of tall trees, and
dust. It was the sort of scene that looked too detached ever
to become familiar, and, in fact, although I did get to know
well the parts of it I frequented, each block of cells with its

surroundings retained its individual seclusion; and there were other buildings whose mystery I never penetrated. When later I had time to wander round the area of the Centre, I was surprised to find that it wasn't given even artificial seclusion from the outside world. It was partially fenced by pierced steel planking used by the allies for airfield runways and fighting vehicle parks, and presumably left behind when the occupation receded from Burma. I saw houses round the perimeter also built of the same material, delightfully airy but hardly weather-proof, and bound to become a mystery to future generations. The fencing gave way in places to a straggly hedge, half-heartedly backed up by barbed wire, but there were several unplanned gaps where access was open from the road, and anybody who wished could wander in and out. Although the surroundings were far from what I had expected, and I was disappointed that my efforts were not to be assisted by the peace and seclusion of my imagined monastery, I realized that I was to do battle with my mind, and that the main distractions would be internal ones that would exist whatever the surroundings. I did, however, hope for peace and quiet in which to practise the meditation exercises: it was quite a shock to discover later that the reverse was the case. Day and night were punctuated by the howling of dogs, bells, and motor horns; and during the day the continuous raucous calls of large black crows in their thousands added to the hubbub. I wondered how on earth it would be possible to meditate in that babel.

But all the impression I was able to gather as we drove to my destination in the light only of our headlamps was of an area similar to a wartime dispersed hutted camp. Suddenly with a final swirl of dust we stopped outside one of the blocks, watched by a few yellow-robed monks who had been walking up and down outside their cells, an occupation I was to be much engaged in during the next three weeks. A pack of a dozen or so mangy and wild-looking dogs of wolf-like appearance challenged us noisily, and then, their duty done, returned to their scratching. I was shewn to the end cell of the block, which was a single-storeyed modern cement building and contained about fifteen cells, each some ten feet by ten. A rather glaring bare electric light revealed a wooden plank bed, a wooden chair and table, and there were two grass mats on the stone floor. I was glad to see that there were two windows (but I soon found out that this was a disadvantage), and was very much relieved to see that the bed was fitted with a mosquito net. The Council had thoughtfully arranged for sheets, a towel, and a flit-gun with a tin of D.D.T. This was to be very much my home for three hard-working weeks, and most of the work would be done within its four walls. It was more than I expected, and I found it easy to visualize it already as 'home'. A naval officer lives much more in one room than most other people, and he soon develops the habit of giving his new cabin his blessing and looking on it with friendly and familiar eyes. In my time I had some that I could never accept, because they were dirty or smelt of oil fuel, or something worse from the selection of smells that a ship provides. But this room was lofty, simple, and clean; and it had a friendly atmosphere about it. I was taken to the bathroom, a large oil drum filled by a tap, a shower, which I gathered was not used, a squatting type lavatory (I was a bit doubtful about this!) and an ordinary seat type that for some extraordinary reason I was told was for 'urine'. However, I reckoned I could sort that one out later. The shower and the seat lavatory must have been a concession to possible laymen students of the type who were accustomed to Western habits. The Chief Executive Officer of the Buddhist Council who had accompanied me arranged to fetch me the next morning so that I could settle all the administrative details of my stay and told me that my first interview with the head monk, Shwesedi Sayadaw, would be at 2.30 in the afternoon. He assured me that if there was anything else that I needed he would get it for me the next day. The party then left, somewhat diffidently I thought, as though they weren't quite sure whether this strange Englishman would be able to look after himself until the next morning!

It was about 9 p.m. I set about unpacking and stowing my few clothes away in a box under the planks at one end of the bed. Then I got to work on the mosquitoes with the flit-gun, and soon had the place orderly and habitable. It had been a most exhausting day, and to-morrow would be one full of test and challenge, and I would have to adapt myself, both physically and mentally, to an utterly strange way of living. But before deciding to start this test off with my plank bed, I spent some minutes refreshing my memory with what was given about the course in the book which had first directed my attention to it and which I had brought with me. I hoped that the task I had set myself would turn out to be simpler than as presented in this book, or I would accomplish little in the three or four weeks I had at my disposal. After a little while I decided to try out the wooden bed. I was being fetched at 5.15 the next morning to be shewn where to get my early morning rice, and this was the last night that I could allow myself more than four hours in bed.

The next morning broke for me well before dawn. My hips were aching and bruised and I had tried every possible way of lying in order to snatch some sleep. I don't quite know why this was, because I had often had to sleep on the floor or on a table in the course of day and night exercises in the Navy where one slept 'on the job'. Perhaps it was partly psychological in that I was sleeping on a bed which in my experience had always been more comfortable than this. Whatever the reason, I was glad to be up at 4.30. I had actually been woken from a short sleep by the howling of the pack of dogs that occupied our quarters, but now everything was quiet, and it was of course pitch dark. I had a shower, dressed, and then sat down to try and quieten my mind from the myriad of questioning thoughts that streamed endlessly through it. It wasn't long before my guide arrived and we walked together the half mile or so to the house within the grounds of the Centre where I was being provided with meals. When I arrived, there were already four monks seated cross-legged at a low table with a large bowl of rice in front of them and several smaller bowls containing a strange assortment of bits and pieces. I was asked whether I would like to sit on a chair, but I declined and said I could manage very well on the floor. But I had a little table all to myself. There was rice for me too, more than I could have eaten in a whole day, and some seeds that looked like lentils but weren't, that were eaten with the rice. Then later came a cup of tea. I didn't really feel hungry at that time of the morning and this meal was far more than my needs, even if I was to have only one other meal in the day, so I arranged later with the interpreter to have only fruit and tea. After this first day I usually had a banana, apple or sometimes papaya, with a pot of tea and a small jug of milk. This, I think, was my only concession to Western habits, besides my decision to drink only boiled water. As I walked back day noises were beginning to take charge of the silence, and there was the expectancy of dawn in the sky, though it was still dark. I grew to enjoy this walk very much, the pre-dawn period has an intimacy that one can share in a particularly vivid way, and for all those who are alone it is a strengthening and enlivening experience. I got into the habit of always stopping in the same place on my return from morning tea, and waited until the dawn broke, while doing an adaptation of the meditation on 'feeling'. It was just by a small lake which lay in a steep bowl and was used by the cattle that wandered around. In the stifling dry days that were to come, I noticed that the level of the water fell a good six inches daily.

On returning to my cell there were the daily chores to be done, making up the bed, and sweeping out the room. I also gave the room a thorough spraying and then kept the windows shut until the sun was up. In this way I kept it free from mosquitoes. Our daily meal was at 10.30, and I had it at the same place as the morning tea. It consisted usually of a large bowl of soup which I found very sustaining although it was more like vegetable water. This was followed by a small piece of fish, or occasionally some meat. There was always rice, which, however, I declined, but I had a small bowl of bean shoots instead. Sometimes there was a piece of Burmese cake or nougat or fruit, and of course the usual tea. This was not specially made for me, the monks had it as well, and with milk in the European fashion. This was our last meal until 5.30 the next morning. One could have as much water as one wanted and I believe tea was permitted, but not milk. I always had a bottle of orange squash in my cell, and drank a good deal between two and six. Although this was much less than I was used to eating, it was quite adequate and I never felt hungry. But since the days were spent in conscious relaxation, and even during walking little effort was expended, it was not only sensible but necessary to reduce one's intake of food in order that the unconscious bodily activities would be reduced to a minimum. During my first meals I was watched covertly by the monks, who ate at the table alongside me, and openly by the wife and family of the man in whose house I was eating. The monks, of course, ate with their fingers, picking up a handful of rice, moulding it with their fingers, and dipping it into one of the sauces and then popping it into their mouth with a final deft flick of the fingers that somehow kept the gravy and rice together. Each monk had a bowl of water and a towel alongside him. I used a knife and fork (another concession I had forgotten to mention). But the novelty of watching me soon wore off and, apart from an occasional small child, I was left undisturbed. The flies and mosquitoes in the house were very bad, and it was usually at this time of the day that I got bitten. Later it got too hot even for the mosquitoes, but the freshness of the morning persisted until ten o'clock, after which the blow-lamp heat of the day started to develop.

A car came for me shortly after eleven, and I was taken to the offices of the Buddhist Council, where I settled the administrative details of my stay. Close by was a huge building which, from the outside, looked like a rocky hill. It was in fact the Council Chamber built in this fashion in deference to the first council which had been held in a cave. Architecturally it is an ugly curiosity, but perhaps the symbolic value makes up for this. The inside is impressive, and when filled with monks and laymen, as it is during the period of the Council's meetings, it would bring to life the dignity that to me is always only dormant in an empty building. My return trip to Singapore had been booked provisionally for a month from this day, but I had always visualized that either I might not be able to hold out for four weeks, or that something might require my earlier return. In order to confirm my booking I had to telephone the airline and it took me three-quarters of an hour. This is not exceptional: the telephone service in Rangoon is, probably because of old equipment, astonishingly bad, although most of the operators speak English. On the few occasions that I had to use the phone, and eventually handed it in desperation to a Burmese helper, I was filled with admiration at the patience with which he persisted. The telephone, which even in England can be the most irritating of modern inventions, in Rangoon is certainly a test of one's power to retain equanimity and patience in adversity!

I was due back soon for my first interview with the Sayadaw, after which the strict routine would begin. And I was impatient to get going. When one is waiting for something that is going to be difficult, and perhaps even unpleasant, the eagerness to get over the period of uncertainty until one knows what it really is going to be like overcomes the dread of starting. It was like waiting to go into the ring, the seconds were out: I was waiting for the bell.

3

FIRST STEPS

THE Sayadaw's house was a little walk from my block, close by the entrance gates to the Centre. It was a modern, square, open-sided bungalow raised well off the ground, and from where I waited for the interpreter who was to take me in, I could see that it consisted of a large single room, at the end of which were silk hangings, presumably dividing it from the sleeping quarter. Presently I saw a puckish figure approaching me and concluded that this must be the interpreter. He was short and of the comfortable roundness of late middle age which was accentuated by the rather untidy way in which the Burmese fasten their longyis. Although the hot weather had not yet settled in, it was a scorching day, and he mopped his face with a large handkerchief every few paces. This was U Pe Thin, and he introduced himself as he came up. He had worked in government service under the British all his life, and, now retired, was the unpaid English interpreter of the Centre. This was no light task, for English was the language that had to be used for all the non-Burmese who came there. These were mostly

Indian, Sinhalese, Siamese, and occasionally Chinese; and as this was, I think, the only Centre for training in the Satipatthana method in the Buddhist world, there was a constant stream of Asian students, and the services of U Pe Thin were called on every day. As well as an excellent command of English, he had a profound personal knowledge of the difficulties to be encountered during the training, for he had devoted regular periods to developing insight through this method of meditation; and he had studied the philosophy on which it was based. He was in fact a wise old owl. I don't know what the Centre would have done without U Pe Thin, and I remember his kindly face with its cheerful grin (unusual for a Burmese) with great affection. He was indefatigable, and his patience in explaining the many points that cropped up during my daily interviews with the Sayadaw was inexhaustible. He was always to be seen plodding round from block to block, handkerchief to brow, on his self-imposed task of giving interviews to the foreign students. It was one of the rules of the course that every student had an interview from a trained monk every day, in which he reported progress and difficulties. This was very necessary, as much to prevent a student becoming discouraged through apparent lack of progress as to help him over the obstacles that would be encountered.

'Are you ready to go in?' U Pe Thin asked.

'Yes, but how do I speak to the Sayadaw? What is his name?'

'Today you will be meeting Shwesedi Sayadaw who has come from Mandalay to look after the Centre and to help you through the course while Mahasi Sayadaw is in hospital. Mahasi Sayadaw is expected back in a few days and he will wish to see you then, but you will probably continue to have your daily interviews with Shwesedi. You won't have to use his name. Just follow me and do what I do.' And with a final mop of his face U Pe Thin went up the steps, shook off his sandals and left them neatly on the top step. I wondered whether there was a protocol for sandals, and whether I ought to leave mine a bit lower down, but decided against it. Inside I saw a thin brown figure seated cross-legged on a large cane-seated reclining club chair: his robe was tucked round his feet and one end of the upper one (for they wear two) was slung loosely over his right shoulder. But at that moment I was not able to get more than a general impression, as I saw U Pe Thin go down on his knees, and with his hands on the floor in front of him, bend down and rest his forehead on them. He did this three times, and I followed suit, feeling rather foolish. But I contented myself with the thought that just as I would salute a senior officer in any of our services, so was this an accepted form of salutation to one who had achieved authority and distinction in his particular service. I never felt quite comfortable when performing this act of obeisance, nor did I feel that it was a very dignified form of greeting.

The Sayadaw and U Pe Thin spoke together for a few minutes, and I was able to study the face of this man who was to be my instructor in a most difficult task. My first impression was one of disappointment. It was not a particularly strong face, or one which radiated serenity. It had, rather, an expression of intensity that may have been an indication of the effort that had gone into the subjection of his mind. It was the face of a scholar and, as with all the Sayadaws that I met or saw, an air of easy authority and a simple dignity was his most striking characteristic. There was nothing in his dress to help this impression: the Buddhist robe is an untidy garment, especially when the wearer is sitting down, and a shaved head is a stark revelation of what character there may be in the face. Although the Sayadaw could understand some English, our conversation was carried on with U Pe Thin as intermediary. At the moment, they seemed to be discussing the general affairs of the Centre, and I settled down as best I could. The thin grass mats did nothing to alleviate the hardness of the floor, and like all Europeans who try the cross-legged position, I seemed to be blessed with too prominent ankle-bones to allow me to sit in this position for long.

The conversation ended and U Pe Thin turned and asked me if I knew the five precepts which were the rules of conduct that I would be expected to follow during the course. These are, to abstain from killing, stealing, lying, and intoxicants, and from unlawful sexual intercourse, and it seemed to me that it would be rather easier to keep these rules here than elsewhere! I replied that I understood them, and would undertake to keep them. There were two other rules, he said, that I would be asked to accept; these were, not to take food after mid-day and not to indulge in singing or dancing. I was tempted to smile at this last provision for our decorum, but refrained because I did not want to give the impression that I was taking the rules lightly; but from what I had seen there was little chance of my being able to indulge myself in this way. In addition, I was advised to avoid all unnecessary talk, to reduce my sleeping to a maximum of four hours a night, and once started on the routine to give up all reading and writing. I was prepared for this and willingly gave the undertaking. The Sayadaw and U Pe Thin then formally recited the precepts in Pali, and I was asked to follow the words if I could, and to accept each precept mentally as I did so. This done, one of the attendant monks handed me a booklet which was a translation into English by U Pe Thin of a comprehensive book on the whole subject of the Satipatthana training written by Mahasi Sayadaw. This gave all the necessary practical details and would allow me to refresh my memory on what was said at the first few interviews.

U Pe Thin then explained that there were two basic exercises to be continued alternately throughout the day. The first was to be done walking up and down either out of doors or in the covered verandah that ran the length of each block. A stretch of about fifty paces was about right, too long a stretch was undesirable because, as will be learnt later, the act of turning was an important part of the mental routine. While walking, the attention was to be kept on the movement of each foot as it was lifted, swung forward, and put down: and each of these separate actions of walking was to be accompanied by saying mentally 'up', 'forward', 'down', or 'lift', 'swing', 'down', or whatever other words were preferred. During each successive step the attention must not be allowed to wander from the activity of the feet. At the end of each stretch the attention must be shifted to the actions of stopping, turning, and starting again. It was pointed out to me (and this was emphasized on several later occasions) that there were two distinct mental processes in each of these actions. First, the intention arising in the mind, and then the command to the body and feet to carry it out. The attention must separate these mental processes so that the action of stopping and turning would have to be done, like the walking, slowly and deliberately.

At the time this insistence on separating the two processes seemed to me to be an artificial one and puzzled me
quite a lot. But I have since come across an interesting statement in a book by D. A. Sholl called *The Organization of the
Cerebral Cortex* which gives a supporting reason for this
procedure. Sholl indicates that separate areas of the cortex
control the desire or decision to move, and the actual making
of the movement. He quotes an experiment by Penfield in
which the stimulation of a particular region of the cortex
produces in the subject a tendency to make a specific movement, but not the movement itself. The object of the procedure was therefore to break the apparent continuity of the
mind and make the subject conscious of the two quite
separate mind actions required to carry out any movement.
The reason for the apparent continuity and the necessity
for breaking the illusion will become clearer to the reader
when the explanation of the Buddhist conception of mind
given in Chapter 7 has been read.

The other exercise was to be done sitting; either cross-
legged, or on a chair, or in any position in which one could
be comfortable and relaxed. The attention in this case must
be fixed on the slight rising and falling of the abdomen that
accompanied breathing. When fully relaxed the breathing
would become slow and shallow, and the movement would,
at first, be difficult to follow. But persistent effort would
enable the mind to detect and hold it to the exclusion of all
else. Twenty-five minutes to half an hour was enough for
each exercise, and they were to follow each other without
pause throughout the day. But if at first I found myself
becoming tense and tired I must stop for a few minutes,
let my mind idle and then start again. The great difficulty
in these simple exercises was the disinclination of the mind

to be fettered in this way, and I would find all sorts of distractions leading my mind away from the business in hand. It was necessary from the start to establish who was the master, and never let oneself willingly be sidetracked into daydreams or other thinking. The matter of distractions is a most important one in any system of meditation, for there are few who can keep their mind undeflected on a subject for any length of time. I was given instruction on how to deal with them at this first interview. The Satipat-thana teaching takes these distractions, so to speak, in its stride, and when they are particularly persistent even makes use of them as temporary subjects of meditation. The effectiveness of the simple method employed soon becomes evident, and introduces the first feeling of confidence that the goal is to be won.

Each time the mind strayed or its attention was attracted by something outside, a mental note must be made of the fact and the mind gently but firmly brought back to the subject of contemplation. In this there was to be no furrowing of the brows, no mental clenching of the teeth, no anger or impatience. Tireless persistence in noting, checking, and pressing on was all that was required. It was the same with the multitude of thoughts that came into the mind uninvited and led one away from the subject of one's task. In this case one had to categorize the type of wandering as, for instance, 'imagining', 'remembering', 'planning', or just 'wandering'. This was a mental note additional to that observing that the straying had been detected, and would bring the fleeting nature of the distraction into contrast with the solid reality of the object of contemplation. When the distraction proved too persistent and refused to be dissipated in this way, then one should turn one's full attention to it, making the distracting noise or the thought itself the subject of contemplation until its force had been expended, when the mind could be brought back once again to the original subject. The thought should be thoroughly investigated, and if possible the reason for its arising discovered. This simple method must become a habit, and as the depth of contemplation increased it would be employed to overcome other difficulties that took the place of external interruptions. In later discussions with the Sayadaw about the various interruptions that were hampering progress, whether it was bodily discomfort, or as I found in one particular case a niggling dissatisfaction with the method, his advice was invariably the same: 'Never mind, just note it and bring the mind back to your subject of contemplation. It doesn't matter how often you have to do this, don't be impatient, in the end you will succeed in quietening the mind and the interruptions will cease.' I found for some time the greatest difficulty in keeping the attention fixed on the movement of the abdomen; it would switch to the breath itself. This was an exercise I had practised for some little while, and it was because it was so akin to the exercise I was now required to do that the attention was so easily diverted. But developing a habit is not the same thing as developing the power to hold the attention under the direction of the will, and all my requests to the Sayadaw to allow me to contemplate the breathing were firmly refused. This was the niggling dissatisfaction that held me back. It was, in fact, immaterial where the attention was fixed. The task was to keep it there. At this first interview, however, I was only given the exercises and the method of overcoming distractions. When this had been done, U Pe Thin turned to me and said 'Now you can go away and start.' I got up from the floor and went out, collecting my sandals as I left. The interview had lasted about an hour. It had been hot in the Sayadaw's house but it was even hotter outside; hot enough for me to make short tacks from shade to shade on my way back to my block. The trees were almost bare of leaf, and the only shade to be found was close in to the cell blocks. On this walk I noticed particularly several monks who were walking up and down in the narrow strips of shade that was all the sun allowed at this hour. I had thought before that they were either aimlessly passing the time, or deep in meditation on some doctrinal problem. Now I realized that they too were thinking 'lift, forward, down', and it was in a way a disappointment to find what a simple task they had, and what a surprisingly inconsequential one! It really seemed too stupid to come all this way to learn the secret of taming the mind only to be told to walk up and down thinking of your feet! But hadn't I heard something about 'washing in Jordan'? Perhaps I should repeat the magic of Jordan in the contemplation of my feet. I had before me some four hundred hours in which to concentrate on my stomach and the action of walking; it was a formidable thought, and I wondered if I could do it. I turned off the path a little and stood at the top of the slope that dipped down to the lake and watched some small boys who were splashing noisily in the quiet of the afternoon. For both the dogs and the crows had succumbed to the heat; the bells too, and the traffic were enjoying their siesta. The heat was ferocious. A few monks who were walking in the sun were shielding their bald heads with their fans. So that was what the fans were for; I must get one too, although I hadn't quite the same excuse.

When I arrived back in my cell, there was already a monk

walking in the verandah outside. This was often the case, and there was usually some competition for the shady side. However, although there were about ten of us in the block doing the training, we managed to fit in our times without conflict and with only occasional navigational difficulties in the narrow verandahs as we passed each other determined not to be distracted from a world reduced to our moving feet. I decided to look for a stretch outside, in the shade of the bamboo behind the block, found a small track and without more ado started off. 'Lift, swing, down; lift, swing, down'. This was easy enough. 'Intending stopping, intending turning, intending starting; lift, swing, down; lift, swing, down.' 'Can I keep this up for twenty-five minutes? But I am already wandering, although that was only a very short break. Here's the end again, stand by to turn. Surely it would be better to walk much longer stretches and reduce the amount of distraction caused by turning.'

'There I go, wandering off again. In fact I never really returned to the subject of my feet, merely congratulated myself on allowing only a short break and then continued the break with another train of thought! You thought you had corrected yourself and then in the middle of the correction wandered off just like someone suffering from oxygen starvation.

'This won't do.' I stopped in order to collect my thoughts once again. Perhaps I was going too fast. I must try walking more slowly and deliberately. 'Lift, forward, down; lift, forward, down . . .

The twenty-five minutes passed quite quickly after all, and I really thought I had been successful in keeping my mind on the job. I had detected little wandering once I had settled down, and it had been easier than I had expected.

The prospect of success was already brighter. Now for the other exercise, and this one must be done in my cell. There was a rough blanket on the bed which I folded up as a cushion for the hard floor. I sat down cross-legged, folded my hands in my lap and spent a few minutes getting used to the position and noticing the movement that I was to follow. It was clear enough, and presently I settled down, to keep my attention on the rising and falling that was apparent against the slight restriction of my longyi. It was not long before the barking of a dog took my attention away, and I was wondering why on earth so many dogs were allowed in the Centre without being properly looked after. Many of them ought to be put down, but of course this would be against the Buddhist principle of not taking life, though I had seen monks eating chicken and other meat at the house where I had my meals. How did they square their consciences about that? The howling of one pack of dogs started off the others all round the Centre, and I could hear them away in the distance like a pack of wolves about to tear something to pieces. How the devil could one keep one's mind fixed with a noise like that going on? I dragged my mind back rather ashamed at having been caught off guard so soon. For the last five minutes or so I had been right off the object of the practice.

There it was again, 'rising, falling', a little less pronounced than before, but still clear enough and exactly parallel with the breathing. I could feel the breath going in and out of the nostrils: that was much easier to follow, for one thing it seemed to be nearer to the mind, though perhaps it was wrong to imagine that the mind operated in the head. But I was being led away again; this would never do; it was the rising and falling movement I must concentrate on, and not breathing. I collected my thoughts once again. And so it went on; hardly a minute passed that I didn't have to check some train of thought that had started unnoticed; and often these digressions had quite a long run before I discovered that I had left my stomach to work on its own. I had never realized how restless the mind could be when it was dealing with something it wasn't really interested in. I must get interested in this rising and falling movement, see if I could detect its start and finish and note its varying depth. After twenty-five minutes of this sort of struggle I felt that I had been shewn up. I must be able to do better than this; after all, I had spent much of my life concentrating on one thing or another with a certain amount of success. However, now it was time for the walking exercise again and only four-thirty. Another seven and a half hours before I could go to bed. That would be eight more walking periods and seven more sitting ones! The practices continued on these lines, with a short interruption just before sunset to close the windows of my cell, and spray it thoroughly. The day had been cloudless, and as the sun went down a last defiant gesture flung a curtain of pure gold over the western horizon matching the spectacular golden domes of the Buddhist temples, one of which I could see from my walking stretch. I allowed myself a few minutes to watch the changing colours of the dying sky; one might have expected vivid colours to fit the dramatic setting of the Eastern scene, but the gold turned to orange, and then to greens and yellows of softest pastel shades, which lingered with the trees sharply silhouetted, until finally these merged into a shrinking purple background, a last faint reminder that the sun had been that way. And presently it was night. So unexpected was this quiet dignified fading of the day, that I often allowed myself the enjoyment of this simple, unadorned spectacle. The dawn was the same. But there were then no clouds to streak the sky with dramatic shapes and colours that spurred the imagination to see a landscape, animals, or giants of an Arabian Night's tale. But drama came as the sun sprang naked from the earth, spreading long, twisted shadows on the ground, and once again the day was here, with its heat and flies and tasks waiting to be done. It was always a marvel to me, and I learnt to watch it impersonally, absorbing the colour and form and light as a simple experience, without connections of any sort.

As the evening wore on and exercise followed exercise, I became tired and restless and it was impossible for me to keep my mind steady for more than a few seconds at a time, until at ten o'clock I felt I had done enough for the first day. The Sayadaw had warned me not to overtire myself, and that strain and tension were to be avoided. A shower in the now deserted bathroom was most refreshing as by this time the water had cooled off somewhat. There were no monks to be seen and I assumed that they were still meditating in their cells, though many of them I discovered later went to bed earlier than the strict routine required. Even the hardness of my bed left me untroubled for a little while, and I fell asleep without a thought of the unusual happenings of this day.

4

THE MIND AT BAY

THE mornings began at a quarter to four. There was no compulsion about this, other than that of my alarm clock, but the Sayadaw had assured me that with the sort of life that I would be leading I would not feel the need of more than four hours' sleep a night; he even went further than this and said that towards the end of the course I would be able to do without sleep altogether. Unfortunately I was not able to put this to the test, for the average person takes about seven weeks to complete the course, and as it turned out I would have only three. But after the first couple of days I found that four hours was ample, and I did not feel excessively sleepy even during the hottest part of the afternoon. But it was advisable not to lie down, which was one of the positions in which it was possible to do the 'rising and falling' exercise! The truth was that one lived a very relaxed and restful day: all the efforts of mind were towards relaxation, and the gentle, ambling walk was no more than enough to ease off the stiffness of sitting. There were days, particularly at the beginning and the end of the period, when I had to give up early and go to bed, but these were usually days when either I had had a lot of pain or a hard struggle with some obstinate feature of the mind at bay. The reduction of eating too, helped towards this relaxation by giving the body less work to do in digesting and eliminating, and the intake was quite enough for the body's needs. The body, so the Sayadaw said, tends to get stuffed up with too much sleeping, as well as eating, and then has to expend energy in overcoming the effects of this indulgence. Whether this would be the case with everyone who seriously followed the routine I don't know, but I certainly did not feel particularly hungry or that I was suffering from lack of sleep.

Once again I was the only one in the bathroom at this early hour. The monks did their washing after the day's meal, between ten-thirty and noon; then they made a job of it, and washed their cooking utensils and their robes as well. In fact they washed in their robes and sluiced water over themselves in the approved Eastern style. I think they were a little shocked when they caught me standing naked under the shower. The sluicing method of washing, though quite pleasant, is messy and wasteful; one monk could half empty our hundred gallon drum, and as the water was usually turned off from about ten or eleven in the morning until sometimes as late as ten in the evening, we were frequently waterless by midday.

The nights in February were still cold, and my morning shower, after a little hesitation on my part, shocked me into the right state to begin the task of battling with my mind again. There was just about an hour before the refreshing walk in the cool of the morning to get my early tea. To start with I particularly enjoyed this walk. For the first few days the moon was high in the sky, the peace of the night had not yet been broken, and I had the feeling that I was a privileged person enjoying something that others were missing. But these walks to the house where I fed, and later to the lecture hall, were soon to become part of the walking exercise, and the concentration on 'lift, swing, down' left little opportunity for enjoying the beauty of the morning. That is, with one exception. I have already mentioned the place where I had turned off the path and stood on the high bank of the lake; here I stopped every morning for a few minutes. It was always just as the light was beginning to break, and exactly opposite where I stood was a tall spreading tree, still in leaf, that gradually appeared out of the dark against the lightening sky. I could savour the gentle breeze as it blew my longyi against my legs and caressed my face and arms; hear the noises heralding the beginning of the day's activities; and see the colour and forms of the trees and houses as they sprang into existence. And I gradually learnt to absorb these sensations without interpreting them in terms of what they actually were, as what might in modern terms be called 'iron-mongery'. I found this very difficult at first, but it became easier as my training progressed. But during those first few days it was a moment of sheer enjoyment of the lovely scene, and a revelation of the power and beauty and the disinterestedness of nature. For the dawn breaks equally for those who welcome it as for those who dread it. It could not be hurried for the one, nor delayed for the other. Its promise was in what you attached to it: the beauty lay in man's senses and not in the significance that he could attach to this particular event. The message of the dawn was to me an impersonal one and gave me the conviction that nature was neither with us nor against us. It is we who pick sides. In these early days I always turned away with a strong feeling that man's intervention in, and so-called mastery over, nature was futile; and I had a fervid willingness to co-operate in whatever way I could. We do not, during our lives, see enough of the dawning of the day, and onset of night; in the cities, the first is recognized only by the start of the traffic, and we only vaguely notice nightfall as we switch on the lights. There is much to be said for the primitive life that gets up with the dawn and goes to bed with the day. As my training developed, the contemplation exercises were extended to cover all my activities and the dawn ceased to be the thing of beauty I first saw, and became merely the ingredients of light, form and sound received by my senses. But in those first few days I learnt to desentimentalize nature without detracting from its value or from its effect on me.

I paused just outside my cell by a bo tree that must have had great significance for the monks in the block, for it was under such a tree that the Buddha is reputed to have been sitting when He achieved final release from the wheel of life and attained Nibbana. But ours was embedded in the hard, stony ground, and its large leaves which earlier would have provided some welcome shade were now daily giving one of us the job of sweeping clear the open space in front of the block. It also housed innumerable crows whose incessant raucous cawing was an additional distraction that had to be overcome. I could, however, imagine a bo tree in full leaf and growing on some grassy slope as a more suitable place in which to meditate than the inhospitable floor and bare walls of my cell. But I must get back to that floor and on with the day's work.

It happened that day that I did not get the welcome

change of walking to the Sayadaw's house for my interview, since both he and U Pe Thin came to my cell at about four in the afternoon. There was little to tell him, except that I hadn't made much progress; but I thought it worth while saying that I had found the walking exercise much easier than the sitting one, in fact much easier than I had expected. The Sayadaw smiled when he heard this, and told me that where there were no difficulties at first they would soon appear. He asked me, rather surprisingly, whether I had had any visions. He repeated this question the next day, and each time when I said 'No I haven't,' I felt like adding, 'and I'm sure I won't either because I'm not the visionary type.' I'm glad I didn't, because I should have had to eat those words! During the interview the Sayadaw again emphasized the necessity of separating the mental intention and the actual command to put each intention into effect. And he gave me a new exercise to switch to at any time when I was having trouble with a particularly restless mind. In this, when either standing, sitting, or lying down, I had to fix the attention on the parts of the body that were touching the ground or the chair or bed. The attention was to be fixed on each part in turn, saying mentally, 'sitting touching' or 'standing touching', etc. In the case of standing it would be the feet only, but in sitting there was usually weight on the feet, the upper part of the thighs, the buttocks, and shoulders; and probably the forearms would be resting on the thighs as well. Each contact in turn had to be made the subject of concentration, and this was to be continued in regular rotation until the mind was ready to return to one or other of the basic exercises.

I now had enough to keep me going for some days, and I felt diffident about having a daily interview when I had nothing to report. It was because of this that for a time I prepared each day three questions on some philosphical aspect of the Buddhist belief to put to the Sayadaw, and these resulted in some very interesting conversations that I will refer to later on. About the second day of the routine I had a bad patch of homesickness for the comforts of my house in Singapore, for a gin and tonic at midday and a whisky and soda in the evening. And for a short time I wondered whether it was all worth it and whether I shouldn't pack up and go back. The monotony was sapping my early enthusiasm and I doubted whether I had the sort of mind that could profit from these exercises, so much better suited to those who lived an existence where time was welcomed as a friend, rather than treated as an enemy to be bested by every sense-tickling device of modern Western life. I could envy them their opportunity, but without changing my manner of life drastically could I benefit from their method? It was the knowledge that ups and downs always beset every new undertaking that kept me from doing anything about it, that and the fact that there was nothing I could do, until the afternoon's meeting with U Pe Thin, and I doubted whether I should then have the courage to tell the Sayadaw that I had given up already. By the evening the mood had passed; perhaps I had had rather more success that day, or it may have been just the process of settling in. Towards the end of my time I became unsettled in the same way, when I realized that I was not able to stay long enough to achieve the full results that the course aimed at, and the anticipation of going back into the world again became a distraction. For a course of this sort one needs to set no time limit in which to accomplish so much but to struggle on until the objective is reached.

During the first week there were some very definite signs of progress that I afterwards learnt are common to all students but which, as I encountered them, were particularly annoying obstructions. The first of these came about so gradually and so naturally that I did not realize that it was anything to do with the practice. I noticed that during the sitting exercise I was being increasingly beset by sharp, sudden, irritations, itchings, and even pains; I always seemed to be scratching or rubbing something and couldn't sit for more than a few seconds without being distracted in this way. I thought perhaps that some of the many insects that inhabited the higher regions of my cell were enjoying the taste of white flesh, and it was only after it had been going on for some time that I suddenly remembered that it was a thing the Sayadaw had warned me about.

There is no doubt that as practice continued unremittingly, the constant checking of the mind's straying started to take effect: first of all I began to detect its attempts to slide away from the subject of contemplation as soon as they occurred, and then gradually the attempts themselves became less frequent. It was this forcible restriction of the mind's incessant activity that introduced the strange phenomenon of the 'aches and pains'. The Sayadaw explained it in this way. While the mind was normally occupied with its myriad disjointed lines of thought that followed each other without break, the pricks and pains that continually occur in the body cannot reach the mind in their individual form; they are received, if they are strong enough, as a general feeling of discomfort; if they are not, they do not intrude on the conscious mind at all. But the continual checking of the mind by the practice of Satipatthana breaks this apparent continuity, and it is then possible for the conscious mind to receive and note each small physical disturbance as it occurs. He would have more to say about the apparent continuity of the mind, but that I must leave to a later chapter.

The 'aches and pains' phase was a definite sign that the intensity of wandering thoughts had been reduced and that these otherwise unidentified impressions were now able to be interpreted in detail. The way to get over them was to ignore them, or if that were impossible, to switch the attention temporarily to the pain or irritation at the time saying mentally 'pain, pain' or 'itching, itching', and it would disappear. When the Sayadaw told me this, I thought such a result was unlikely, but it did indeed happen just as he said. It encouraged me no end to find that I had reached one of the signposts that proved I was actually progressing towards my goal. This phase soon passed. There was however one pain that I was unable to overcome in this way; it was in the region of my heart, and was at times so severe that I had to stop the exercise, and occasionally I was forced to lie down. I reported this to the Sayadaw and he repeated his instruction. The pains were often severe, he said, but they would disappear if I persisted, and I must pay as little attention to them as possible. But for days I was held up by this annoying symptom and no amount of concentration would dissipate it. I eventually came to the conclusion that it was an abnormal pain, probably caused by muscle strain. The cross-legged position in which I always sat, and that meant some nine hours a day, was not one to which I was accustomed, and keeping the spine straight in this position would inevitably throw a severe strain on muscles which would not be developed to take it. I decided in future to spend one period each in the morning and the afternoon lying on my bed doing the 'rising, falling' exercise. This cured the trouble and I had no recurrence of the pain, but it held me up for a week or more.

No sooner had this phase passed than another started, and this was a very cunning trick that the mind played. Once again I did not realize what had been happening until it had been going on for some time. When the mind strayed in its normal straightforward manner, it did so in words; that is, the new thoughts came into the mind in words, and the business of straying continued with imaginary conversations, or just word thinking. I hadn't actually realized this at the time, but that was, in fact, what happened. Suddenly, without my noticing a change, instead of thoughts in words, pictures flashed into my mind. When I eventually discovered what was happening and looked back to see when it had started, I remembered the first picture very clearly. I was walking along a dusty road when an old man came up to me, knelt down and offered me a bowl of soup. It was just a momentary flash, but startlingly vivid, and I was quite taken by surprise by this strange action. The whole thing was just as inconsequent as a dream, but I knew I was awake and it appeared convincingly solid and real. There were many like this before I realized what was happening. In another particularly vivid one, I was driving my car along an unknown road and another car passed me. As it passed, the driver turned and looked at me. His face was sharp in detail, not as a face would be that was moving past me at speed; it was a stationary face. I noted the features carefully, as I seldom if ever do in a dream, and was once again surprised to see a look of complete unconcern as though he had nothing to do with the car he was in. In dreams one is not surprised at the strange things that happen; but in each of these mind pictures there was something unusual that caused me surprise. The unusual thing about these pictures, which I had never experienced before, was not only the vivid detail that I observed in them, but that they appeared absolutely real. But they were only flashes, like stills from a film, and whatever the action was that I observed, it happened without prelude and remained frozen for the period of the flash. They provided, of course, a magnificent opportunity for the mind, which seized on some particular aspect of the picture and was away on a long follow-up of fancy thoughts quite unobserved!

These were, of course, the visions that the Sayadaw had so persistently asked me about, and about which I had felt so scornful. But here they were, so real that at first I could not believe that they hadn't actually happened. I would not have described them as visions, but I suppose it was as accurate a description as any. Once I was aware of what was happening and watched out for being led astray in this way, they were detected and dealt with, just as the word thoughts, and they didn't trouble me for long.

There was just one other minor difficulty that came along a bit later: this I described to the Sayadaw as 'toppling'. All these things seemed to happen during the sitting exercise, and in this case I found myself gradually leaning further and further forward until I lost my balance and the upper half of my body toppled forward. This would occur at frequent intervals, and each time I was brought back with a start to my physical position and surroundings. The Sayadaw explained this as being a sign that I was approaching 'Samadhi', that is, a state of intense concentration, and he said it would pass. I must try to deal with it without disturbing my contemplation of the body, by switching my attention momentarily to the action of the toppling, followed by the conscious action of righting myself again. This was not easy to do, but the funny thing about all these interrupting phenomena was that as soon as I had been given the explanation of them and tried out the method of overcoming them, they soon stopped.

After the first couple of days, the Sayadaw suggested that I could, if I wished, do my exercises during the very hot part of the afternoon in the lecture hall. This was a large, empty hall (for when it was used everyone sat on mats on the floor), generously provided with overhead fans in regular rows. By selecting the right switches I could arrange to have the fans running above my walking stretch, and over a pile of mats where I had elected to sit. Without this very modern equivalent of the shade of the bo tree, I don't think I would have had much value from my afternoons' exercises. I had my interviews with the Sayadaw in the hall too, and he seemed to welcome the relief that the fans gave just as much as I did.

This hall, with its large image of the Buddha behind a glass screen at one end, contained some puzzling relics of British rule in Burma. I have already referred to the cane-backed reclining chair that I saw in the Sayadaw's house: I thought this was perhaps some legacy that the Sayadaw had adjusted himself to. But there were several more of them in the lecture hall, and both during my interview and whenever the hall was in use, monks sat, rather uncomfortably I should have thought, on the sloping cane, with their legs tucked under them. I knew these chairs well for I had seen them in all the British clubs East of Suez: they were designed for the after-lunch siesta, and under each arm was an extension piece that could be swivelled round to form a leg rest. True, it resulted in a picture of the white man that one hoped did not go further than the club boys, but then the after-lunch siesta was never a very dignified affair. The Sayadaw had no idea that the extensions existed, or why the chairs were like that. I suggested that they had been removed from the clubs when the Centre was being furnished, but he said no, they were being produced by a firm in Rangoon. It was a useful demonstration of the different use to which an almost symbolic element of British Colonial rule could be put. It was symbolic to me too, of the often misplaced enthusiasm with which we imported Western democratic ideas to countries where the structure of the community was not ready, or the psychological background fit for it. I hoped that where such organizations had been retained in countries that had achieved independence, there would be found as effective a compromise as in the matter of the chairs!

One day towards the end of the first week Mahasi Sayadaw returned from hospital and I was taken to him for my daily interview. He looked ill and tired, but he impressed me immediately as a man of remarkable presence. He was tall and strongly built, and his face of almost classical lines had an eager look that was in contrast to his unwavering, penetrating gaze. I felt that here was a man of great understanding and sympathy, and one who could have no narrow conception of truth. I was encouraged to think that he might welcome my questions, and that I would not have to be content with formal doctrinal answers. There was none of the drawn look of the ascetic about him. His was a face that radiated strength, confidence, and serenity. The typical Burmese face is round and full, but the faces of all the older monks I saw seemed to have been lengthened by their meditative efforts, and this gave them a stronger cast and better balance of feature than was apparent in the general public. Many of the monks were extremely good-looking men. I don't know how old Mahasi Sayadaw was, but his face was without wrinkles: there was a sympathetic stillness about it that was, to me, immensely impressive. I felt enveloped by an authority that sprang not from ordering, but from being. The dignity that was so apparent in all the Sayadaws was an obvious product of the lack of conflict between the physical and spiritual man, and the complete-ness with which their whole nature was dedicated to living in peace, and in confidence that the path they were following would lead them to release from attachment and desire and to achievement of the final goal of Nibbana. It was not at this first interview that I began to put to the Sayadaw the questions that led to such interesting discussions. On this day he obviously wished the interview to serve only as an introduction, and I appreciated very deeply his action in seeing me so soon on his return. But there were later interviews that took place in his house, as he had now taken over again from Shwesedi. The latter however remained on at the Centre and still undertook the main part of my instruction. Although many of my meetings with Shwesedi were hilarious affairs, he was on the whole far more diffident in answering my questions. I think he was a little disconcerted at having to deal with a European, while Mahasi, who was a more experienced teacher, was far more at home with the idiosyncrasies of Western thought, and for that reason his answers were fuller and more satisfying.

My life had soon settled into the rather monotonous routine of walking, sitting, walking, and inevitably in the process the outside world began to recede from my conscious thoughts. I shall discuss in the next chapter how the progressive steps in the meditation exercises were intended to close one's horizon in, and to keep one occupied within a clearly defined field. As the world outside the Centre and my immediate occupations became less real, the small, insignificant details of the day's events round my block assumed an importance that has left them standing out in my memory with quite disproportionate clarity, when compared with others before and after my visit, that were of far greater import. It is the degree of attention that etches depth and permanence into memory and not any intrinsic value of the event itself. Looking back on the experience now, it seems as isolated as the time in which a man might be looking at a slide through a microscope, or the heavens through a telescope, though in both these cases there is sufficient interest within the confines of the instrument to encourage and retain the attention, while in the life at the Centre the limitation of the object of attention was achieved by ensuring continuity of the occupation of the mind within a very clearly defined sphere. It was only gradually that this limitation became effective, but that it did was conclusively demonstrated to me when, in my third week, I had to telephone the Australian Embassy in Rangoon to reply to a cable I had received from Singapore. In thinking about the cable and arranging to telephone I felt that I was being rudely torn out of my environment, and it was with a sense of acute excitement tinged with apprehension that I spoke on the telephone giving my instructions to the Naval Attaché. When the business was finished and I walked back to my cell, it was with a feeling of relief that I felt the material world shrinking to the immediate precincts of my cell block, and consisting once more of the monks, the dogs, and crows, and the heat and mosquitoes of my cell; all things that I had managed to fit into an orderly and unruffled existence. But it took a little time before the disturbing wave that had been set up was fully stilled.

5

THE SATIPATTHANA METHOD

THE theory behind the Satipatthana method is simple and logical, and I am sure that the analytical Western mind would feel much more confidence when embarking on exercises of this sort if the explanations that I shall give in this chapter were forthcoming. But they would not normally be given: it was a case of 'do this, and you will experience that; not necessarily at first, or even soon; but in the end, if you persist'. I had, as I have already said, read a little about the method before going to the Centre, but most of the explanations that follow were obtained in answer to my questions at the interviews with one or other of the Sayadaws. At first, Shwesedi was reluctant to give me answers that were not actually needed for carrying out the practices or overcoming obstacles, but he relented when he saw that it was not mere curiosity that prompted me, but a genuine desire for an understanding that would increase my confidence and support my persistence. This reluctance to embark on theoretical discussions is common

Buddhist practice, and I shall have some more to say about it in the next chapter.

The Buddhist object in undertaking a course of Satipatthana is to obtain 'vipassana' or insight. It is only when the mind has been stilled that the insight, or as we might call it, intuition, can gain access to, and reveal as experience, the facts that form the basis of the Buddhist doctrine. It is because of this revelation that the Sayadaws are reluctant to talk about things that in any case cannot be properly understood without experiencing them, which with a little patience and perseverance each man is capable of doing for himself. Moreover, these spiritual experiences are interpreted differently by different people, and it is most difficult to explain such a thing without giving a new significance to words commonly used in other contexts, or coining new ones without being able to explain exactly what they mean. The truths that are experienced by 'vipassana' are those that are necessary for a proper understanding of Buddhist thought and to enable one to follow the Buddhist way of life with the conviction that comes from full understanding and not just blind faith. This is an approach to religious belief to which we are not accustomed. Acceptance is based on experience and not on faith.

During his long ministry of forty-five years the Buddha repeatedly told his followers that release from rebirth, desire, and suffering was available to all who would follow the 'way of mindfulness'. This 'way' has been condensed in the course of Satipatthana now taught throughout Burma. There are many forms of meditation about which instruction is given in the Buddhist scriptures, but this particular one points directly inwards, and works by clearing away the dross within *from within*, instead of employing love, compassion, and selflessness to make contact with the spiritual basis of man *from without*. That the Buddhists deny any permanent entity in man must be mentioned here: it is the most difficult tenet of Buddhist thought for a Christian to understand; but I must leave discussion on this point to the next chapter.

I had as my object in taking the course rather less than this revelation from within, for I knew that with the time at my disposal it was most unlikely that I would make sufficient progress to enable me to experience it. But I did hope and expect to learn whether it was a course that was suitable for the Western mind, and whether the ability to pin-point the mind and hold it steady for long periods was one which the average man could be expected to achieve. As far as this hope was concerned I was at the end fully satisfied that the course was simple, safe, and logical, and that there was no reason why any individual should not reach the limited goal I had set myself.

The first important requirement in the task of learning to control the mind was to restrict its activity. Conscious control of the mind is under any conditions a difficult thing to achieve, but if during the attempts to do this the mind is allowed its full field of operation, it is impossible. It must in some way be restricted. We do this unconsciously when we are particularly interested in a thing to the exclusion of all else; and if effective restriction can successfully limit the mind's activities over a long period, it is possible for the will gradually to assume control. The whole secret of the success of the Satipatthana method lies in the selection of a natural field for these activities which, though restricted, offer the mind continuous occupation.

The two basic exercises that I was given at my first

interview were the beginning of this restriction process. I have mentioned earlier that the simple, sensuous pleasure that I derived from my morning tea walks had to be given up to the contemplation of the movement of my feet for every step of the way there and back. Very soon the actions of eating were included in the contemplative exercises. The mind had to follow the movement of the hands and arms in lifting the food to the mouth, and the actions of chewing, swallowing, and drinking. Each consecutive action during the meal, from the first one of sitting down to the final wipe of the lips and getting up, had to be followed consciously without break. The greater the amount of detail that could be included, for example, tasting, and the feel of the cool water in the mouth, or the actual texture of the food that was being eaten, the easier it would be to keep the mind from wandering. It was not really as difficult as it sounds, once the initial disinclination to accept the task had been overcome. After this, the actions of getting up in the morning, washing, etc., and going to bed at night were added. It very soon became a habit to make my first conscious thought in the morning 'waking, waking' followed by a quick run round the senses to detect the touchings, sounds, etc., that they were receiving. Then came the action of sitting up, stretching out first one leg and then the other, getting out of bed, standing and so on. Each action of washing followed: stretching out the hand to turn on the shower, feeling the water on one's body, rubbing with the soap, drying, and then on the walk back to my cell 'lift, swing, down', until one arrived at the door, when actions of stretching turning and pushing were necessary to enter the cell. It can be readily understood that the mind was indeed kept busy, and this close attention to all the bodily actions continued until one or the other of the basic exercises was started. In this way the mind was given little chance of finding its way back to the outside world, and it was left with a sphere reduced to the immediate vicinity of the body. The effect of even the first attempts at this full restriction was quite remarkable: the mind was at all times fully occupied, but always with things, so to speak, just under its nose! There was no time of the day when it was not following the immediate physical activity of the body. Even such things as coughing, scratching some insect bite, or blowing the nose (and this became an early lesson for me, for I seemed to have a continual cold and occasionally long bouts of hay fever) had to form part of this day-long contemplation of the body. The day that began with 'waking, waking', ended with 'lying touching', following round the points of contact that the body had with the bed, until sleep intervened.

This was the full restriction that the Satipatthana method required, and its effectiveness lay partly in the fact that it made use of a field of activity that was of the most intimate concern, and also in the ease with which it could be progressively introduced. As the new habit of thought was being developed, so the walking and sitting exercises continued throughout the day: it was only in the short intervals between these that 'body thinking' took over. There was one other variety allowed to the mind in this day-long contemplation, and that was the particular mood or feeling of the moment, if it was one for which classification was clear, and particularly if it were likely to intrude into and handicap the exercises. As the principle in this case is the same as in the body contemplations I need not enlarge upon it. A mood of elation or depression was noted consciously by saying mentally, 'I am in a mood of elation or depression.' A few moments spent contemplating the mood in this way was usually enough to prevent it interfering with the normal exercises. The term 'mindfulness' of course implies a watching of every activity that the mind and body embark on, and this sensation of being a watcher became strong as the continuity of 'mindfulness' improved.

By now, although the mind never gave up its attempts to stray altogether, the tendency was noticeably less, and it was detected and recalled with greater ease. Its scope had been limited so that the temptations open to it were fewer. Now the task of keeping the mind steady began seriously, particularly during the sitting exercise, which was when physical activity was reduced to a minimum. The action of keeping the mind on a movement that was a product of breathing had the effect of slowing the breathing itself, and this in turn made the movement shallower. The mental effort required to follow it became at the same time finer and finer, until it employed only a minute portion of the mental potential. It was when a balance was finally achieved and the mind stood poised, but effortless, and wholly receptive, that the opportunity for insight, intuition, or awareness to enter would occur. But first the mind took advantage of this quite appreciable reduction of physical activity to evade the control that was gradually becoming effective. Day after day it continued its tricks and got away on some interesting topic of its own, and each time it was brought back. Just when you felt that in a series of exercises one morning you were nearing the final fixing of the mind, the afternoon's exercises would show you that the end was nowhere near in sight, and the mind was as frisky as ever. There were days when I felt that I was losing ground and told the Sayadaw so. But he inevitably replied, 'That is to be expected; don't worry about it, just continue to check the mind, gently and firmly, without impatience or irritation, and in the end you will succeed.' And in the end I did. Like the beam of a lighthouse, the mind locked on to its subject of contemplation and remained with a stillness that excluded time. Although it was the will that had put it there, there was no sign of it when the stillness had supervened. This stillness now had to be made secure, and a thing that could be recalled again and again, until a track had been opened up through which insight could reach and flood the conscious mind. This stage, to my infinite regret, I did not reach. But that it would have been reached I have no doubt whatever.

In one of the discussions, the Sayadaw gave me the reason why intuitional awareness is so seldom able to reach the conscious mind. In our normal life, although we may think we are directing the mind consciously from object to object, in reality there is continually a fringe of 'butterfly' thoughts whose activity is quite uncontrolled. These thoughts will intrude into the conscious mind whenever they are able, and inevitably as soon as the mind relaxes they successfully crowd out the intuition which holds back for a quieter and more orderly entrance.

We really only half believe in intuition, which by men is considered responsible for the inconsistency of the female, and by women as a sign of their inherent superiority. But, in truth, it is available to all who consciously encourage and develop it. It is, however, in most of us a rare, uncertain, and timid process, that can so easily be edged out by the more pressing thoughts of our immediate concern. But once the ability to clear a passage for it has been developed, this awareness can become a familiar state. It will be received as experience, and not just as information about things; as a 'knowing' that comes from a contact with the 'known' that somehow short-circuits the five senses: and the confidence that accompanies its content is of a startlingly different degree to that we associate with the knowledge that is absorbed in the normal manner.

Associated with this restriction of the field of the mind's activity that the Satipatthana method imposes, is an attempt to accept all sense impressions in the form in which they are received by the senses, and to avoid all interpretation of them by the mind. It is these mental constructions that are immediately applied to each sense impression that lead the mind away from its attention to the bodily activities. The noise of a bell is at once recognized as such, and a bell form visualized; the direction from which the noise came is immediately added and the fact that it probably came from a temple that had been seen with its pagoda scintillating in the late evening sun follows. All this happens without any apparent conscious effort to analyse the simple sense impression. To accept the impression as it was received meant that one had to try to leave the sound simply as sound and not allow the mind to start on its sequence of interpretations. This could be done by fixing the attention on the sound IN THE EAR and following it until it faded into silence. The same thing had to be done with smells; and with the contacts revealed by the sense of touch, though in this case, whether it was the breeze on the skin, or the clothes on the body, it was necessary to bring to the attention things that otherwise would have passed unnoticed. I have already mentioned my daily pause by the lake in the early morning; it was here that I spent ten minutes running over the sense impressions that I was receiving, and enjoying the new intimacy of their simple reception without the contaminating effect of constructional analysis. It was so natural to classify a noise as 'temple bell ringing', and having learnt all there was to know about it to discard it quickly from the mind. But now I became far more intensely aware of the characteristically golden-toned singing of the temple bells that lingered on the air until it was a gossamer thread of sound. It filled the whole of my awareness, and became a part of me; until, as it finally faded in the ear, I felt that I was losing a cherished possession. It was a source of wonderment to me to find how much pure enjoyment I got out of simple things of which previously I had been barely conscious. And I found a new appreciation of all sound and touch sensations, and even of sights, though this was a far more difficult sense impression to catch before interpretation had muddied its magic. It was however just possible to do this at that time of the morning when the light was only beginning to make the mind active in interpretation. In front of me across the lake, the hazy tree remained a form, and the colour as it gradually appeared, was colour, and not leaves and branches. I found that this practice gradually gave a much deeper significance to sense receptions, particularly of sound and touch; and at the same time I felt a primitive enjoyment that was free of associations and without reason.

This effort to retain sense impressions in their purity, as it became a habit, was a first line of defence in preventing the mind from straying, for it limited the straying to the simple message that the senses gave when a distracting noise or feeling arose, and since this was still the immediate vicinity of the body, attention could either be temporarily switched to follow it, or the mind more easily recalled to whatever subject it had been concentrating on. My morning exercise by the lake was not in fact one given me by the Sayadaw; it really developed from my attempts to restrict the mind to the physical activity of the body, but it received his approval when I had managed with some difficulty to explain through U Pe Thin what I was doing. Rather naturally there was strong discouragement for a student to undertake any exercises other than those prescribed for the Satipatthana course.

It was desirable that a monk should do this course in 'mindfulness' at the beginning of his training, or as soon after entry to the order as he had learnt the elementary ethics of his new life. This is a significantly different procedure to our normal method of learning. We give the mind little attention on its own, but try to stuff it with as much information as it will hold, in the hope that it will in some unspecified way turn into knowledge. There is admittedly an intention of training the mind along certain regular tracks by selecting the information to be absorbed; but much of our learning is equivalent to the stuffing of geese to produce *pâté de foie gras*. The Buddhists, on the other hand, start by tackling the mind itself and training it to allow access to insight. The teaching that follows then continually encourages the uprising of this insight in the form of understanding, or knowledge. This is manifestly putting the horse where it belongs, and does not leave it to find its way between the shafts by climbing laboriously over the cart! It is in the matter of interpretation that scholarship is needed, for without the words and the knowledge of how to use them, the sense of one's experience cannot be conveyed to others. But this comes later, and is in the main only undertaken by the senior monks and

Sayadaws. Even if the aim of a course of learning is not one in which insight could play a part, one would have thought that the training of the mind in some such simple way as this Satipatthana method would ensure that the tool employed was being made to work efficiently. In order to prepare men and women for the increasing technical complexity of modern industry and the various government services, we give them courses in every conceivable branch of activity. Particularly in the fighting services a man tends to progress from one course to another, and there is no doubt that an early training in Satipatthana would both reduce the time required for these courses, and narrow the ever widening gap between information and knowledge. I had the impression, though the Sayadaw never specifically said so, that he regarded much of what we in the West call learning as information that does not lead anywhere, and very often results in the sense of a thing being lost in a mass of irrelevancies. What is strange, is that we follow the principles employed by the Buddhists in our technical undertakings. We would never allow such inefficient operation of a machine tool as in the case of the mind we accept without question.

The discussions I had with the Sayadaws on the Satipatthana method greatly helped me to understand what I was trying to do, and gave me the confidence that enabled me to continue when little or no progress was apparent. But these explanations were a concession to one whose mind had been trained in analytical methods: it was normal to confine the course to 'doing' and to exclude the reasons. This is the faith aspect of the Buddhist teaching, and is in contrast to that of the Christian: the one is 'do this, and you will learn to understand' while the other is 'believe this, and you will have the promised benefits'.

6

NO SOUL, NO GOD

I HAVE already mentioned the difficulty I had in getting the Sayadaw to answer questions other than those directly connected with the practice of Satipatthana. I found this reluctance and occasional direct refusal to give me any sort of an answer rather disconcerting. But the habit I formed of preparing each day three questions that had direct bearing on the thought behind the practice did in fact bring me a certain amount of information; and it is from this that the subject matter of this and the next chapter is derived. It was with Mahasi Sayadaw that I had the most interesting discussions; he was, I think, a little more prepared to take a broader view of what was applicable to my study of Satipatthana, and he was obviously well versed in Western philosophy, at least so far as it conflicted with Buddhist thought. Both he and Shwesedi became far more forthcoming in discussion towards the end of my period of training. The main topic of our conversations was the working of the mind, and something about this came up most days, as it was used to illustrate why the difficulties I was encountering had occurred, and how they should be dealt with. But I was seldom able to draw them further than simple elementary explanations of their thought. Neither is it easy to find much about the Buddhist theory of mind in their voluminous literature, because references to it are scattered throughout a large number of writings and discourses, although I have since come across significant passages that fit the beginnings of the understanding I found while at the Centre.

There is, of course, good reason for this disinclination to indulge in philosophical discussions or to give explanations beyond those that are absolutely necessary for carrying out the meditation exercises; and it is strictly in accordance with the Buddha's instructions. During His long ministry He persistently refused to answer certain questions, and most skilfully turned His enquirers' attention to the unhelpfulness of either knowing or not knowing the answers, pointing out that they were not matters that would lead to the cessation of suffering. It is clear from His discourses that His method was first to develop spiritual stature and the capacity to understand, so that the searching mind would find the answers to its questions in the experiences that followed the practices. Had He wished, the Buddha could have formed, during the forty-five years of His teaching, an inner core of men highly trained in the deepest content of His thought, and fully capable of understanding it. But this He did not do; and it must be assumed that He deliberately withheld the knowledge He had, in order that there should be no risk after His death of followers being able to acquire information that would have no matching experience.

There is nothing more productive of dissension than

attempts to describe the deepest spiritual truths and experiences to those who have not themselves experienced them. For they cannot otherwise be properly understood, and will inevitably be distorted to suit the hearer's particular degree of comprehension. In order to pass on knowledge, a teacher must be qualified, and this qualification is of two kinds. He must first of all have intimate experience of the particular aspect of truth he is teaching, and he must have the necessary intellectual development to enable him to interpret the experience in terms that others can understand. If the interpretation is successful, understanding by his hearers is in fact recognition of something they have already experienced. If it cannot be received in this way it is merely information and not knowledge. One is met over and over again in the Buddha's discourses by a deliberate deflection of questions the nature of which would not contribute to the struggle for release from suffering and the wheel of rebirth. These are the 'silences' that have caused so much comment and difficulty to Western students of Buddhism. But although they have always been accepted by Buddhists, it is possible that the very silence itself can lead to misunderstanding, and this may have indeed occurred in the case of the question about continuity after death. An answer, to those who were not aware by experience of the structure of man, could have led later on to different versions of the explanation that would be diametrically opposed. But it is possible that even the silence that the question elicited has been misunderstood. It is perhaps the most significant characteristic of Buddhist teaching, this strict adherence to the example of the Buddha in not giving explanations of spiritual truths until they can not only be understood but recognized, and even then allowing no effort to be expended on matters that would not directly assist in the struggle for freedom from the 'toils of rebirth'.

A policy of withholding or disguising the deepest spiritual truths must be followed by every spiritual reformer if he is to avoid the dissension and strife that follow from different understandings of doctrine. Without experience, an affirmation of certainty is worthless; with experience, it needs no emphasis. We have good evidence of the harm that compulsion to believe dogma can do, in the bloody wars that have traced the history of Christianity. The ministry of Christ was a very short one so that comparatively few heard the teaching direct from His lips, and too many people have since added twists of doctrine about matters they thought He ought to have included. But we can see in the homely explanations and descriptions of the qualities that would lead men to God, the same desire to reach the simple understanding of His followers and to avoid the distracting temptations of philosophical discussion. This is most beautifully illustrated in His reply to the question 'Is it lawful for us to give tribute to Caesar, or no?' His teaching was mostly in parable and in the father-son parallel. In such a short mission His message had to be simple and direct to be grasped quickly and easily, and to avoid the likelihood of being misunderstood. But unfortunately, the simplicity of His message did not suit those who had not had personal contact with Him or His immediate followers, and the addition of a mass of irrelevant doctrine led to confusion and worse. Some of the bickerings that have resulted from differences of opinion about matters on which Christ never touched in His teachings have been so ridiculous that they could only have sprung from a complete misunderstandng of Christ's message. It is strange that the followers of the

Buddha's teaching have persistently refused to enforce the belief in doctrine and only indicate how to reach understanding and experience of its content, while the followers of Christ have persistently done the reverse.

But to return to the difficulty of drawing Mahasi Sayadaw into discussion. There were so many matters which I felt were related to the training I was undertaking and on which I needed something to set against the well set logical reactions that my mind was trained to give. The questions I asked mainly concerned the Buddhist understanding of the nature of mind and its relation to the physical body; the doctrine of Anatta, which has come to be understood, as the denial of the soul; the Buddhist conception of rebirth; and the relation of mind to time. On two of these matters I got nowhere, but when I found that Mahasi Sayadaw was prepared to give me some simple explanations that he thought me capable of absorbing without disturbing my practices, I developed my questions in small progressive steps, and it is in thinking about his replies subsequently, with the help of the result of my meditation exercises, that it has been possible to reach an understanding of mind and time that I believe is in line with Buddhist thought, and which I have not yet discovered in the literature of the West. It is to a brief description of what I feel should be the true import of the Anatta doctrine to a non-Buddhist, and an attempt to explain a new way of regarding time, that this and the following chapters are devoted.

This very difficult doctrine of Anatta, which is the central pillar of Buddhist belief, puts the individuality and personality of man in a very different light to that normally accepted by the West. It is a drastic elimination of something that has become for us as much a counterpart of our existence as the solid ground under our feet, and at first there seems to be nothing to put in its place. It took a long time for the young Christian to believe that there was anything to him but the body. In the years from childhood to maturity the body was paramount. The beauties that inspired him were brought him by his senses. The material world was obvious, compelling, and satisfying. Why should one have to believe that there was something behind it all, and something in oneself that could not be seen or, to tell the truth, even detected? And yet there was at the same time an inner urge to believe in something deeper and of finer substance than the solid earth we saw around us, a desire perhaps to avoid having to classify ourselves as being as transient as the rest of the physical world, an awakening fear of insecurity, and even of the futility of objectless existence. It may have been all of these things, or it may have been the spiritual nature of man beginning to seep through the material coverings. But in anticipation of these feelings of inadequacy, Christianity offered us a soul. Here was something that opened up an escape from a purely bone and muscle outlook, however unspecific it might have been when we first met it. But it was difficult to grasp, this conception of something so intangible, so inaccessible, and mostly so shy. The convincing acceptance of it by our elders induced us to take it for granted, to give it the regular encouragement our spiritual advisers recommended, and without having any really first-hand experience of it, to accept it as an unobtrusive and comfortable partnership and an insurance against the possibility that the physical body might not after all be the total of our existence. And so gradually a belief in the possession of a soul as a rather ill-defined internal appendage became a firm characteristic of thought. Now one meets this doctrine of Anatta (which after all is believed and understood by millions), and this comfortable substratum of gentility is under fire. There is no soul; no permanent entity in the human being.

On this matter there was no reluctance to tell me what I would come to understand. Buddhist belief rests on three foundations of fact about our human existence. These are, Dukkha, the universality of suffering; Anicca, the constancy of change, everything is transient; and Anatta, the lack of any permanent principle or entity in the human being; all things are without a 'self'. I was constantly being reminded of these facts, presumably in order to enable me to relate them to my mind, which formed so large a part of my 'self' as I knew it, and about which I was daily learning new facts. But these were the only elements of Buddhist doctrine that the Sayadaws or U Pe Thin ever referred to without being prompted. Dukkha and Anicca gave me little to think about, for although suffering is not usually accepted by us quite in this light, it is, from experience, a legitimate (though without the Buddhist solution somewhat pessimistic) way of regarding existence. That all things are transient is, I think, not open to question, and one does not have to be a Buddhist to believe it. But with Anatta I had difficulty. I had from an early age been acquainted with Hindu beliefs, which stemmed from the ancient Brahman faith, in which the Buddha was probably well versed; and here the 'I' formed the centre and spiritual reality of the individual, surrounded by layers of varying material grossness. The dispersion of these layers and freedom for the 'I' could be found by following the disciplines now widely understood as Yoga. The similarity of one of the Yoga disciplines and the Buddhist is heightened by the one fundamental difference, Anatta, and it is worth considering how the one works before trying to work out what the other means. The Raja Yoga method of self-analysis consists of a process of stripping the components of individuality and personality to see which can be identified as the 'I'. Beginning with the various parts of the body. If I cut my arm off, is the 'I' reduced? If I lose my legs, is the 'I' affected? and continuing until it is clear that no part of the body constitutes the 'I'. It is entirely independent. Then sensations, emotions and thoughts are in turn scrutinized and discarded in the same way. The 'I' is not there. Finally a still centre is reached, where certainty resides without describable attributes. This cannot of course be achieved simply by an intellectual, analytical process, but each stage must be made the subject of persistent meditation. Having discovered by this method the existence of an 'I', the next stage is to expand it to include the 'I' of every other being, and of every manifestation of creation. That the first 'I' discovered by analysis and meditation was still an illusion of separateness has to be realized as imperfection, and must be overcome in the final struggle for union with the absolute.

But the Buddhist attitude is unequivocal. There is no 'I', no self. Why should the Buddha have introduced this significant change in his prescription for attaining Nibbana? Was it possible that in the method of the Brahmans there was a dangerous tendency in the analytical process to produce a glorified sense of 'I' of immensely increased power and purity, which however would bring its own temptations and hindrances to further progress? Whatever the reason, there is no doubt of the necessity: without having discovered for himself the non-existence of a 'self', a man cannot be a true Buddhist. But this discovery will lead him to other difficulties. The Buddhist, as the Brahman, accepts rebirth as part of the process in which spirit learns to disentangle itself from its material prison; but if there is no self what is it that is reborn? And what is the point of rebirth if there is no continuity of an 'I' to press on to fuller expression of its true self and final release? These questions I asked Mahasi Sayadaw, but received the reply I have already mentioned, 'You will understand all this if you persevere with your meditation.' But the doctrine of Anatta, devoid of any explanation of what was to be understood, I could not accept. It seemed such a depressing and pessimistic outlook and really reduced the individual to something of no significance. I told the Sayadaw that until I had received enlightenment through my efforts I must be accepted as an 'ego' amongst the 'ego-less'. And this became quite a joke. My greeting, when I presented myself for examination in the afternoons, was frequently 'Is the ego any less ego-less today?'

Though I was unable to give the matter any serious thought while at the Centre, I have since. For as I then understood the statement it did not fit in with the highly mature thought I found in the Buddhist beliefs. I felt that there must be some way of looking at the relationship between the individual and the power behind the universe that would explain why so much emphasis was put on this negation of what was an essential belief in other religions. Millions of deeply thinking men could not accept a negation that appeared to be purely destructive. No soul, and no God. I was certain it could not mean what I understood by those words. And there I believe lies the explanation. It doesn't. Words can be the very devil. If we were unable to speak there would be far less misunderstanding. With all the civilization that language has brought, some good, some bad, nothing has been more productive of discord than the belief that it is possible to transmit abstract thought accurately by language. The fact is that no two people speak the same language; and in speaking about spiritual matters, words like God, soul, spirit, where they are not just familiar sounds, have widely different meanings for each person; and to explain them, other words must be used, which are equally lacking in precise meaning. Most of us still retain as the basic understanding of such words the picture images we were given in our childhood. The thought of soul is still in some way related to the picture of a figure with wings dressed in a long white robe. And God, from being a communal father, has grown in attributes rather than in conception. We like to see our thoughts in pictures, and feel that to think of God as a principle leaves us without care and protection and eliminates the thought of love between creator and created, while at the same time we are guilty of *lésé majesté* to God Himself (even the word Him immediately misdirects our thought). We are afraid of depersonalizing God, and are able to find no picture to put in the place of the paternal ruler of the universe. But in reality this should not be impossible for a courageous and mature mind. We do it with other words, particularly those used in science such as electricity, and magnetism, where our understanding is satisfied by the effects that the principle produces in our daily life. By relegating God to the picture book we fail to find Him in the world around us. The strong hold of childhood's teaching usually prevents us from reassessing the meaning of words that require introspective thought, and interpretation of personal experience with the adult resources of the mind.

To deny then the existence of 'an individual soul' and of 'God' is no more than to deny that the current interpretation of those words, either at the time of the Buddha's mission, or now, helps to lead man to his spiritual goal, whether it is Nibbana or Heaven. The Buddha constantly refused to give his followers a precise interpretation of words, the meaning of which could only be indicated in parable or allegory. At best it would only relieve curiosity, and at worst it would be likely to hinder man in his striving for release from change and suffering, and from his domination by desire. The Buddha's attack, as has been that of other spiritual reformers, was on the 'self' and the illusion of individuality; and all the disciplines of the Buddhist way are set relentlessly to develop the knowledge that overcomes the sense of separateness. It is natural that the full development of this attitude would consider that merely to introduce a higher form of 'self' or permit the retention of any form of 'I' would prove a stumbling block to final deliverance. Nothing must be interspersed between man and the distant horizon, and nothing must be allowed to cloud the truth of how deliverance was to be won. Complete negation of 'self' and 'I' was necessary. The sense of 'I', of individuality, as anything other than a temporary illusion would foster all the ills that are the natural result of considering oneself and others as separate. Spiritual progress in any discipline will lead us through brotherhood to oneness, but this final goal, however it may be described, is a step that requires a new awareness born of a new experience. It is no good teaching it in words. It can only be learnt by experiencing it, and this the Buddha said would happen if man followed the path He laid down. In this path the intermediate 'I' of the Raja Yoga analysis did not have a place.

And so the Sayadaw was in fact saying to me 'I can give you no answer that you will understand, until you find it for yourself by reaching a new awareness in meditation'.

But at the risk of being misunderstood, there are some thoughts that can help to put the 'no soul, no God' doctrine in a framework that is neither agnostic nor unchristian.

God is not to be understood as any personification of power, but as the ultimate reality behind all forms of life and matter in our universe, and in all other planes of existence. Such a reality cannot be parcelled out in separate bits, though what is called 'the descent into matter' produces the illusion of a myriad of separate entities of very greatly varying densities. The degree to which the reality or spirit within its material cover can be detected is shown by the emergence of what we call spiritual qualities, and these are the qualities that follow from a gradual reduction of the sense of separateness. The various material coverings that disguise the reality of the spirit can be thought of as windows of varying opaqueness, through which the underlying reality can be observed, but it is in each case the one indivisible spirit that is being observed, not an individual separate element of spirit. If we were able to see and understand it in its entirety, it would be like looking out of the window of an aeroplane and seeing the limitless expanse of cloud above which it was flying, instead of looking at the window and observing only the small individual picture of cloud it presented. It is the covers that present the illusion of separateness, and from this illusion stems all the ignorance in the world. We call this ignorance evil.

Spirit, as a separate entity, cannot be the subject of reincarnation, for its separateness is apparent only as long as the material envelope exists to clothe and mask it as an individual. Spiritual progress is the gradual stripping away of this material envelope until finally the appearances of individuality will have gone with it, and spirit will be apprehended as it is and always has been—the only reality, where nothingness and allness meet and are the same.

But what then is rebirth? What is it that is reborn? Do all beings cease to exist when they die, and are new individuals constantly being formed?

These questions can only be answered satisfactorily if it is accepted that the law of Karma rules throughout creation, and is, so to speak, the moral mechanism through which the layers of materialism surrounding the spirit are discarded. This law requires that each cause must have its effect, and that all causes shall be fully worked out. The energy created by every thought and action must be absorbed and expended in others which in turn create energy to produce further reactions. Some of this energy tends to assist the stripping-away process of the material coverings from the spirit, and some to reinforce and increase them. We ourselves and our present circumstances are the result of what we have done and thought in the past. We shall be the result of what we think and do now. No act or thought dies stillborn, but each produces its train of results that continue until the original energy is expended. And so we develop ourselves for good or evil through our own actions. This is surely high justice: there is no evasion of the results of our bad thoughts and actions, or failure to secure the effects of our good ones. But the way in which we react to the events they cause can help to dissipate the energy, or to recharge it. This law therefore makes of every individual a collective group of potentialities for good and evil, for tendencies of all kinds, and for the joys and sufferings of his present and future existences. These constantly changing potentialities, held together perhaps in some envelope of matter finer than anything we are aware of, forms the entity that reincarnates. There is nothing permanent about this entity, and at each rebirth the working of the spirit behind the enveloping sheaths of materiality can be observed just so much. But one cannot imagine the same portion of spirit to be enveloped each time, there is no parcelling up of the spirit in this way, nothing to be defined as a soul that follows the envelope of 'unworked-out causes' on its journeys. The spirit is always everywhere, but it can only be perceived here through the medium of physical creation. We are windows of the spirit, and our previous thoughts and acts determine the degree to which the spirit can be observed through us. In working out our Karma we hope to rub a little of the dirt from the window during each existence, until, when the window is finally clear, personality has gone.

This I believe is the real meaning of the 'no God, no soul' doctrine so firmly held by all true Buddhists. It is not a deadening, but an inspiring, belief. God is not denied, but conceived with vastly greater affirmation. The soul is reinterpreted as a temporary, changing, and eventually vanishing entity, with the whole oneness of spirit without conceivable attributes behind it forming the reality we but dimly perceive. The personality that lies with the group of cause and effect energies seeking fulfilment has continuity during the long process of setting the spirit free, but it is constantly changing, and is doomed to extinction. It cannot be called a soul. And the spirit that works through it is an undifferentiated part of the ocean of spirit we call God: it cannot properly be called 'a soul' either.

A great many people in these days are dissatisfied with the interpretation of God that Christianity gives us, and with the lack of clear explanation as to what the soul really is. Most clergymen behind the convenient cover of God as a superman probably hold their own maturer idea of how God should be thought about. They will, however, meet the difficulty of having to continue to present the God of the Bible to their parishoners, many of whom will be perfectly content with the 'father' qualities. Thinking so easily becomes a habit that the effort to work out for oneself a new and more satisfying conception may well be over-weighed by the necessity of being loyal to the old. Most of us, on the other hand, do not have the opportunity or the inclination to rethink our conception of God, and our relationship to Him—soul; and we can neither accept the teaching of the Church as adequate nor find easily a new ready-made conception elsewhere. This difficulty of placing ourselves in a satisfactory relationship to reality lies, I suspect, at the root of the materialistic outlook that is so prevalent today. And there is no easy solution. For a ready-made reinterpretation is not the answer. If we have, to our own knowledge, passed the stage where parallel and allegory are sufficient, then there is no means of gaining new understanding except by working for the experience and awareness that will give it substance.

7

SOME THOUGHTS ON MIND

THE most valuable contribution to my understanding of
the Buddhist conception of mind came as a result of the
'pricks and pains' I have mentioned in an earlier chapter,
and which I complained about to the Sayadaw as interfering
with my meditation practices. The result of my bringing up
this comparatively insignificant hindrance surprised me,
for I did not expect to be offered such a simple solution,
but rather exhortations to ignore it. This uncomfortable
distraction was however itself a sign that my mind was
beginning to react to the control I was trying to develop,
and it is a symptom that helps to demonstrate the way in
which the mind works. This was an occasion when I found
it very difficult to follow U Pe Thin's interpretation of
Mahasi Sayadaw's explanation, and it was necessary to
cross-question him about the precise meaning of the terms
he used; in this way it was possible to draw him out a
little into giving me somewhat more than was absolutely
necessary. We were, as on other occasions when my
examination took place, in Mahasi's house, sitting on the

floor, not cross-legged, but sprawled rather untidily in front of Mahasi, who was as usual sitting cross-legged on his club chair. I could never get over the incongruity of his informal 'throne', which was in such contrast to this tall, dignified figure, whose golden brown shoulders were bare but for a fold of his upper orange robe flung lightly across the left side, and whose shaved head fitted the stern impassivity of his expression. It was, I thought, the quiet sternness of great understanding, and not of rugged and relentless self-discipline. He often smiled during our conversations and sometimes laughed.

It was very hot, and my hands left wet patches where they rested on my longyi. Neither U Pe Thin nor I ever managed to sit in the traditional cross-legged position on the hard wooden floor: I still needed a rug or cushion of some sort to prevent my ankles from going to sleep, and U Pe Thin had spent too much time sitting on office chairs to be as naturally comfortable as were the monks and others less practised in Western habits. I found myself constantly shifting position, as much to relieve the excessive dampness of the parts of my body that were touching each other, as to find some position of my legs that would fit the floor with less discomfort.

The onus of beginning the conversation was always with me, as I was expected to report the progress I had made or the difficulties I was encountering. At first I had been hesitant about reporting things that seemed to be of very minor importance, always expecting that there would next time be some significant progress or a difficulty of a magnitude worth bringing up. But Mahasi had encouraged me to talk about my practices, and I soon learnt that the most unexpected and valuable help could result from discussing some quite insignificant attitude, habit, or experience. So, on this particular day, I had decided to report on the annoying little bodily discomforts that had only recently become apparent, and which were bedevilling my every attempt to sit still for a few seconds at a time. Even now I felt that I was almost reporting for the sake of having something to say, for it seemed such a stupid little matter which one ought to be able to grapple with oneself. In this, however, I was wrong. It is a well recognized symptom that all who practise experience in the early stages of reducing the mind's activity. I was, I admit, at first somewhat sceptical of the Sayadaw's explanation of the phenomenon, and his recommendations for overcoming it; but I realized that I was dealing with the totally unfamiliar, and the very fact that the Sayadaw not only wasn't in the least surprised, but filled in details that I had omitted, gave me the confidence to accept these, to me, very ordinary pricks and pains as something very out of the ordinary indeed.

The mind, so said the Sayadaw, is without any inherent continuity: it is not always bearing thought; and it is not a form of unceasing energy. We normally understand it as always containing thoughts, our thoughts, which follow one another in rapid succession, without pause or gap between them. This is partly true, as being our experience of how our mind functions, but it is not true of the nature of mind itself. It could be considered as a stream consisting of minute fragments of mind each containing some particular thought. Mind acts as the medium for thought as canvas does for the painted picture. But each element of mind with its thought is entirely separate and disconnected. This stream of particles of thought appears to flow past our consciousness unceasingly. But it is only unceasing because we make it so. Our thoughts are connected to one another by memory, inference, desire, attachments such as our likes and dislikes, cravings and fears, etc.; and it is these habits and attitudes that link each minute element of mind to the next, so that it seems to be an endless stream of thought pressing for attention. During our waking hours there is no indication of discontinuity whatever; our minds are continually occupied. Even when we speak about their 'being a blank', what we really mean is that we were day-dreaming, and not conscious of our immediate surroundings. The attention is faintly engaged on some fleeting thought, or some worry unconnected with our present activity and environment.

The commonly supposed ability to 'make your mind a blank' is something that in fact few people can do without long training in mental practices similar to those of the Satipatthana course. But when we dream, several curious things happen to this stream of thought, because the connecting links are not so firmly under the control of habit or influenced by our environment. Incidents do not necessarily follow each other in normal waking sequence, and the lack of logical connection does not surprise us. We dream that we are going upstairs with the object of entering a particular room, and suddenly we are inside it without ever having gone through the door; or we flit from place to place without any of the inconvenience of travelling! Moreover our judgements are at times quite extraordinary and we do the most unusual things without being a bit surprised. The bridges that normally join thought to thought and which, in our waking hours, we insist should make a nice tidy logical sequence of thoughts are no longer working so effectively; and what we see as a pattern made to fit all our accumulated prejudices when we are awake, becomes in dream disjointed, non-sequential and altogether different. In deep sleep thought is totally absent, and so—but this is anticipating a bit—is time. When we have been sleeping really deeply we have no idea how much time has elapsed; it might have been a couple of minutes or some hours. In dreaming sleep on the other hand we retain a sense of time, which is however as capricious as our dreaming thoughts.

This stream of really isolated thought particles appears to us to be a long connected succession of thoughts, and if we like we can unravel the connections that lead from one to another. These are sometimes clear and obvious, but often lie below the surface of the conscious mind—some memory or association, or perhaps a sharply felt fear or wish now faded and forgotten. It is sometimes necessary for the technique of psycho-analysis to be employed when deeply buried thoughts are causing psychosomatic conditions. But whatever the connections may be, they can generally be classified under the heading of what are understood by the Buddhists as 'attachments'. These are the things that are related to the self through some need, craving, or desire. And of course such things as hate and fear come under this heading, as they are usually caused by desire, and are the reactions which the immature self produces when frustrated, or made to feel insecure. Now the Buddhist plan of salvation, or reaching Nibbana, is through developing detachment from the self; and this is won in two ways, by the path of morality as presented in the scriptures, under the eightfold path of right understanding, right thought, right speech, right action, right livelihood, right effort, right mindfulness and right concentration; and by the gradual negation of the self through meditation practices. But this must not be understood as a positive process of negation; it is rather the discovery of the illusory nature of the self as it was known before, and a positive process of expansion towards the goal of unification and release. Both of these methods attack the root of attachment—the self, and in this way the number, degree, and power of the attachments are reduced. There is therefore less inducement for one thought to follow another, and gaps begin to occur. The particular branch of Buddhism that is called Zen employs drastic techniques to bring about the same result. The monks are given seemingly nonsensical questions and statements to meditate on, and when they ask questions of their masters receive unexpected, illogical, and sometimes active answers, accompanied by striking or belabouring with any handy object. Zen masters frequently deliver sermons that, to us, appear to be meaningless or even the ramblings of a disordered mind. There is nothing to grasp; nothing that can be referred, inferred or related; nothing on which the mind can get to work in its accustomed manner. And that is just the point of this sort of madhouse procedure. The whole process is intended to break the long acquired habit of logical thinking, of the necessity for proceeding from thought to thought along well defined habitual paths. The mind is made to untrain itself; to think without attachments, in fact to learn to isolate individual thoughts. The result is that when success comes, it bursts through during some quite inconsequential discussion and quite independent of what the discussion may be about. Illumination is suddenly won as a result of all the efforts to deserialize thinking. The stream of thought has been broken, and a gap has occurred which has allowed the intuitional awareness of truth to break through. That is why in Zen literature the monk is always shewn as seeing the light at the most unexpected time and without having made any apparent progress towards enlightenment. He asks some question such as 'Where is peace and the end of the quest to be found?' and receives the uncompromising answer 'The dusty hen's egg rolls over the rocks.' And immediately he sees the truth and understands all and goes away satisfied. This is not a true example, the question and answer are mine, but equally fantastic ones are common and can be found in any of the Zen literature. We may fail to understand how such childish behaviour can possibly lead to spiritual illumination, but the whole training of Zen, with its hardships, its physical hurt, and its pointless disputations is designed to put an end to the domination of logical reasoning, and to produce gaps between thought, through which the light of knowledge can enter. Its particular merit is that it is frequently the quickest path to knowledge for those who can willingly undergo the discomforts. It is not a gradual process, but a stark struggle ending in a joyful bursting into freedom without prelude.

In the gentler step by step progress of the Satipatthana training it was the first beginnings of 'the gaps' that I was experiencing.

I have in Chapter 4 given the Sayadaw's explanation of how these gaps are seized on by the normally subconsciously received sense impressions of the many minor discomforts that constantly assail the body; and of how these impressions are now able to get into the queue of thoughts being presented to attention. The very fact that they appear in what is, so to speak, an empty space, gives them greater emphasis, and all the normal reactions of the body's mechanism respond to deal with these magnified pin-pricks. Concentrating on them temporarily reduces them to their proper proportions of insignificance; and as the will becomes more successful in keeping the mind on the subject of meditation there is less and less chance of these low intensity impressions getting through.

It was exhilarating to become aware of this reduction in the uncontrolled flow of thoughts, and when I went back to my meditation exercises after the Sayadaw's explanation, I immediately realized that I was experiencing mind as the Sayadaw had explained it to me. Perhaps it was just that his explanation had helped me to realize what was happening in a way that fitted the facts. I felt, however, that I had received such an important piece of information that I allowed myself an hour that evening to clear my mind about the afternoon's conversation. I had really so very little to work on, but what I had heard was new to me, and I wanted to find out whether it would fit other conditions of our existence as well as the difficulties of meditation. It was then that I found it fitted in with the curious antics of the mind in dream—the Sayadaw hadn't himself referred to this, though he had hinted that there were times when we were unable to force a logical sequence on our thoughts. I began to see, too, that this conception could have a very clarifying effect on our personal relationship to time.

There was much I wished to clear up by further questions, but I knew I was not likely to be successful, and might make the Sayadaw regret that he had given me so much already. I had only been given a description of mind, with its thought content. What was its condition before it had been brought into active existence by thought? Was it in a position similar to the potter's clay before it had been given form at the hands of the potter? Each thought only made use of a minute portion of mind, and a great many of these 'loaded bricks' never came within the sweep of the conscious mind; the stream seemed to divide and take two routes, one presented itself to the conscious mind and the other apparently opted for a quiet life, unobserved elsewhere. That these thoughts appeared to be trapped in some cases was shewn by the repressions, often revealed by psycho-analysis. Perhaps if our conscious minds were less burdened with unnecessary thoughts there would be fewer tucked away in our subconscious unable to escape. It is this coming to the attention of the conscious mind, and the presentation in orderly sequence, that gives us our impression of personal time. The apparent flow does not depend on any quality of thought-loaded mind, it is from the act of attention to each thought, combined with the artificial connections we make between them that we get our impression of an unbroken sequence of thought flowing past at measured speed. So the processes of thought are intimately connected with our personal sense of time and duration.

It would have been interesting to have learnt more of the nature of the attention we give to each thought; simple and obvious as it may appear, this quality of attention is fragile, unpredictable, and only developed by haphazard methods in our Western education system. We all have occasional demonstrations of the obstinacy of attention to do what it is told. A very remarkable example is an experience that often occurs on waking from a dream. At the exact moment of waking the dream is clear and indistinguishable from waking experience; but as one tries to fix the waking attention on it, it fades rapidly, and all effort of will is unable to recall it. One has a feeling of impotence as the once clear facts of the dream swiftly recede and are lost in the distance beyond the reach of our waking thought. In a few seconds, nothing can be remembered of it at all. We are very conscious of the fading process and however hard we try to capture the content of a perhaps exciting dream as it fades, it is no use, the attention cannot hold it. And for good reason; since it is being bludgeoned to respond to all the inrushing messages from the wakened senses, and we are not sufficiently in control of the attention to tell it to ignore them. Because the whole of the Satipatthana training is developing the control of attention, I had hopes that I would be able to recall these fading dreams and hold them for survey, by the waking mind. But I was no more able to do this after the course than before.[1] The attention during dream acts in a very rarefied atmosphere; the distractions it encounters are few, and if serious, which is seldom, they either enter into the dream or waken us. Attention in dream is held much more lightly than it is by the comparatively crude presentations of our senses when awake. It is toying not very seriously with the fleeting idle thoughts of the dream state, and the coarser waking attention, attuned to much more solid impressions, cannot find enough on which to grip. It would have been interesting to have got the Buddhist views on matters of this sort, but neither of the Sayadaws would be drawn further.

There was one problem which I felt was so important that it was worth putting up as one of my 'three questions', and I mention it because it produced a most interesting and surprising answer. The question was this, 'What is the connection between the mind that thinks and gives orders, and the physical brain that carries them out in the body;

---

[1] It is possible that the reason for this lies in the difference of intensity with which we follow our dreams and our waking experience.

and how does it work?' I repeated this several times to U
Pe Thin with additional explanations of what I was after,
in order to be certain that he had got the question right; and
I then watched him pass it on to Mahasi Sayadaw with
what seemed to me a somewhat anxious look on his usually
cheerful face. There was no hesitation about the answer,
it was, 'Mahasi Sayadaw cannot answer this question since
the Buddha never considered it and has given no instructions about it.'

I persisted. 'But the Sayadaw has obviously given much
thought to these things, and I would be most interested to
hear what his own views on the matter might be.'

At this U Pe Thin laughed, and replied without waiting
to pass my remark on to the Sayadaw (but the latter understood most of my English; he was able to read the language
well but I never heard him speak a word). 'The Sayadaw,'
he said, 'cannot possibly give you any opinion about a
matter which has not been included by the Buddha as one
for instruction; it would be impossible for him to have an
opinion on such a thing.'

Neither Mahasi nor U Pe Thin was aware how baffled
I was by this reply, which naturally ended the conversation.
It was a shock to discover that a man whose mind was keen,
highly trained, and superbly mature, a mind accustomed to
penetrate to the core of problems few Westerners would
have the patience or the ability to tackle, could be bound by
a doctrinal rule of this kind. There must be here, as in the
case of the Anatta doctrine, some explanation that is bound
up in the meaning of terms. I don't believe such a mind
could exclude knowledge of such an important fact as the
relation of mind to the human body, though I fully appreci-
ate that it might be knowledge that he would be incapable

of passing on to one with only a fumbler's understanding and too much information! The only satisfaction I was able to take away with me was that the answer to the question would not in any way help me to achieve 'samadhi', the stage of complete concentration; or to find 'vipassana', the insight that brings knowledge; or finally to realize 'Nibbana'. In fact, the rule here was 'keep your eye on the ball'.

I would be surprised, however, if there were not a fairly simple answer to this question; simple that is, provided the question is asked in the right way and all the links in the chain of which the answer must consist can be understood. So often when a question in science or in philosophy is unanswerable, it is really that the framework in which the question is set precludes an answer, anyhow of the type one is looking for. This particular problem is one which I think will be solved before long, by inference at least if not by demonstrable fact. Much is being learnt at the present moment about the functioning of the brain, which might almost be described as a highly complex electronic machine, in which minute electric impulses constitute the messages that lead to response in the body. There is developing a parallelism between some of the products of the new science of Cybernetics and the latest theories of the processes that occur in the brain. There is also from other sources some evidence to suggest that the mind can exert a force that can have physical effect, and I do not think it is stretching the imagination far to accept that this is possible. In fact we may shortly have to accept mind as an extremely tenuous form of matter. Apart from our natural dislike of departing from the solid foundations of matter, that we see and feel around us, this should be no more difficult than believing

Einstein's discovery of the shrinking of matter in the direction of motion when measured from a stationary datum. We are quite accustomed to thinking of, and indeed dealing daily with, matter of greatly varying densities, and we find no reason to draw an arbitrary line between such things as lead and hydrogen, although the latter is not visible to us, and to the majority of us scarcely even detectable. There seems no reason why we should decide to limit what we call matter to what is at present identifiable by today's instruments, though in all truth this has become tenuous enough already to give the simplest molecule in comparison an elephantine solidity! It would be a bold (and unimaginative) scientist who would not feel that there must be degrees of matter even finer than anything we have so far been able to detect. Such matter would be able to produce visible effect by impinging on matter of the next higher degree in the scale of density, until it entered the relatively crude field of our awareness. This happens with the gas that works a refrigerator, or with the atom in an atomic explosion that helps to decimate a town. It might be that mind in this way is able to affect the very small electrical potentials that exist in the brain, and thus bring about the changes that we require in the body. It would be easier for me to accept some explanation of this sort than to believe that a non-material mind can cause effects in a material brain. Here again, of course, we are up against the difficulty of what words really mean. For I have expanded the term 'matter' to include whatever mind is made of, without in any way finding out anything about mind that would justify this. But are the present boundaries we set to matter justified? Isn't it just a case of what matches our perception; and the finer we can make this, the finer the degree of matter we shall discover? The discoveries of science are made in the main by looking for something our minds have thought of, and only rarely by examining something our instruments have discovered. It may be that the problems we are facing now require us to accept mind as being within the field of matter.

8

ON DIMENSIONS AND TIME

Most school-children of today will speak of the fourth dimension with familiarity. It is time. It is no longer a mysterious something with which to stimulate the imagination in an adventure novel. It has been ousted by space-travel where scientific ingenuity and physical activity in the face of unknown odds are the ingredients; the tricks that time can play have lost their novelty; the few plays and books that have traded them to the public have had little impact recently; they have come too late. Time, we feel, has been masquerading as a mystery, but it has been exposed, and now as the fourth dimension it is as easily accepted as the propositions of Euclid. Of the complex thought and manipulations of symbols that led to this exposure we care little; that sort of thing is the proper concern of men like Einstein and others who are adequately equipped by scientific training to expose the myths and legends believed in by our grandparents. Exactly how it comes to be the fourth dimension, and what difference it makes to our understanding of ourselves and the universe we inhabit by being so, is a matter into which few enquire; for part of the fact of time being a fourth dimension is obvious with but little thought, and it is apt to escape our attention that there is another side to this conception with which we are vitally concerned. It is part of our awareness of existence, and as such has a very personal characteristic that is very different to time as measured by a clock.

In order to clear our minds about the matter, it will be worth while developing as simply as possible what is easy to understand about time, as it is commonly used in mathematical and graphical calculations.

It may come as a surprising reminder that no 'thing' (and I use this term in a very literal sense as a physical thing) can have existence unless it possesses the maximum number of dimensions of which we are aware.[1] In our earliest experience of geometry we learnt that a point has no magnitude. It therefore has no existence except in imagination, and only then when imagination is being hazy and skating round the conception without coming to grips with it. A line has length but no breadth; it can therefore only exist in the imagination in the same way as the unfortunate point. We next learnt that an area has length and breadth, but no thickness, and is equally something that cannot exist. Finally we reached the volume that has length, breadth, and depth, and was therefore considered, and would still seem, in the common-sense view, to be solid enough to exist. But it can still only exist in the same sort of woolly imagination as the point, the line, and the area, for it has no continuity: unless it possesses the dimension of time, it exists for no measurable duration and could be perceived in

[1] This would appear to be an axiom that applies to all creation as we know it, that is, all creation in our plane of existence.

no way and by no means as a 'thing'. It can come into existence only in our newly found four-dimensional universe. This is as simple an explanation as any of the need for a fourth measurement, a measurement in time to give all objects substance.

Let us see what there is to be learnt about time by analogy with the way in which these progressive dimensions have been developed. We can imagine (though without any concrete visualization) the dimensionless point moving and tracing out a line, which can be said to have been 'created' in this way: and we now have one dimension. In a similar manner the sweep or movement of a line at right angles to itself 'creates' an area with two dimensions, and the sweep of an area at right angles to itself 'creates' a volume with three. If using the same words we take this process further we would say that the sweep of a volume at right angles to itself produces an object in our universe. But what can these words 'at right angles' now mean? In each previous case it refers to a direction that doesn't yet exist. The sweep of a line to produce an area is in the direction of its thickness which is non-existent. We are in each of these three cases of the point, the line, and the area introducing a new conception which can neither be deduced nor conceived of within the limits of its own dimensions. So that 'at right angles' really means 'out of its world', and it is the movement or sweep that is absorbed or represented by the next higher dimension. The line becomes an area through movement, and we become real through movement in time. In order to reach the point of view of the next higher dimension we must develop an awareness in which the last added movement ceases to be regarded as such, and is perceived as the whole of a new dimension. It is because we have not quite grasped this conception that time seems to us to be such an unusual sort of dimension; it appears to be breaking new ground, to be a somewhat highbrow kind of dimension. But in reality our perception of volume is of the same character. We know it by the awareness of touch, of its feeling of solidity; and when we see it we imagine this. But we have been brought up inaccurately to think of ourselves as three-dimensional beings, and our extension in a fourth dimension has never seemed to be necessary for our reality. Now we have been 'brought up with a round turn' to realize that as three-dimensional beings we are just as unreal as the point, the line, and the solid. The right angle of our new measurement is the extension in time that is absolutely necessary for the real existence of any object in our universe. This direction is not inherent in the three-dimensional volume.

All is now clear and tidied up. Perhaps it is, about the particular consideration of time that we have been making. But is it the end? Where does this process of extension cease? What is to prevent somebody discovering a fifth dimension, which will then require that everything in order to have real existence in our universe must possess five dimensions, and that this new dimension must be thought of as an extension at right angles to time? I am not here suggesting any sort of similar conception as Dunne's 'serial time'. This new extension would be something 'out of this world' and bear no relation to any kind of time. Such a discovery may well be made, and I believe that eventually a full understanding of the mechanism of our awareness of time will bring it about. It is possible that before long we may have to consider existence in another plane as being essential in order that four-dimensional existence as we now know it can have substance; such a new plane of existence could well be considered as an extension at right angles to time, fulfilling in every way the requirement for a fifth dimension. However, we need not consider further this possible development here, though it will be necessary to refer to it later in order to round off our thoughts about time.

The way of looking at time that we have just followed is entirely analytical. It can be, and is, most usefully represented on paper in graphs, and by symbols. Time as a co-ordinate soon became familiar to us in elementary mathematics, but it is not perhaps thought of clearly as being an always necessary dimension that must be added to the other more orthodox three in order to give real existence to anything.

There is another way of approaching the problem of time that should be of far greater concern and interest to us. What we have been discussing is a purely academic dimension that applies as much to a stone as to a human being. But, unlike the stone, we have ourselves, or we think we have, a sense of time—something in our nature that gives us the ability to differentiate between past, present and future, and an unshakable conviction of the direction from one to the other. In fact we have a quite distinct though not very consistent awareness that I have referred to in the preceding paragraph, which we feel is linked to academic time and which we have just selected as recipient for the honour of being the fourth dimension. Unfortunately there is no parallel on which we can draw from the other dimensions that would help us to understand how we should think about this awareness. There are, to the best of our knowledge, no two-or even three-dimensional beings; and if we with great difficulty try to imagine ourselves as flat beings having only length and width and living completely within a flat surface, it is impossible to imagine what sort of awareness it would be that would give us the clue to the next higher, the third dimension. But it is an interesting exercise in imagination to try this out. We would be existing entirely within a plane surface, with no knowledge of an 'above' or a 'below', and no idea of how to think of what these terms might mean. We are utterly bound by the flat surface in which we exist and in which we feel we have complete freedom in every possible direction. We shall just have to assume that if such a being were able to experience his whole plane of existence being moved at right angles to itself, it would be as some sort of awareness of it as is our awareness of time. His physical senses will be entirely unable to detect it, just as our senses cannot detect time. But if a three-dimensional being could observe the situation, he would immediately recognize this movement as being in a linear dimension, and the awareness that the two-dimensional being has of it would be understood as the sense of detection of thickness. It is highly unlikely therefore that our awareness of duration is anything more than a purely personal reaction to something that is in reality a measurement of a quite different sort.

Let us for a moment look at some of the vagaries of this sense of awareness of time or duration that we take so much for granted, and which is of such significant importance in our daily lives. It will be interesting to discover whether we can look at it from any standpoint that will help to unveil its illusiveness. In the first place we must dissociate our thinking from time as represented by a clock, which is only a measurer of academic time, the co-ordinate of the graph transformed into a more social guise. We shall consider only time as we might know it in a dark room where day and night are the same, and where our senses can find no indication of the measurement of clock time other than what is inherent in ourselves. There are occasions in our normal daily lives when we can rely on our sense of time to a very reasonable degree of accuracy, but this usually occurs only when we are engaged in normal non-intense activities, the undertaking of which gives us a good indication of clock time. At the same time there are all sorts of other indications that are unconsciously added to this— the fading light, the noises of traffic, even the habits of eating (not to be mistaken for the pangs of hunger!). All these things add up to give us a fairly accurate time sense. But if we are reduced to the simple existence of the isolated dark room and are without any of the outside helps to indicate the passing of clock time, even our stomachs will give us no more than an indication that we are hungry, that might be described as 'stomach time'. In such a situation our only guide is the amount and manner in which thought has been passing through our minds. This might be considered a most unreliable yardstick; it is in fact a measurement of our own personal time and will seldom bear much relation to clock time. We all know, without perhaps thinking much about it, that when we are deeply engaged on some subject, or with some single thought, clock time will fly: our attention has been steady and the normal flow of thought that gives us an impression of passing time is absent. On the other hand, when our thoughts are churning over, changing rapidly from one subject to another, or reviewing some matter from constantly changing angles, or even constantly repeating thoughts of the same kind, as when we are worried or anxious about something, a long time seems to have elapsed. A state of anxiety or worry is in strong contrast to one of deep, steady concentration where attention is fixed. In the case of a worrying thought, the attention, like a butterfly repeatedly revisiting the same flower, stays for a moment, doesn't like it and moves away, only to be drawn back again to the same nagging thought. The activity is equivalent to a succession of different thoughts about the same thing: our consciousness is full of change, and clock time lags. When in our dark room we are experiencing a rapid succession of lightly held thoughts, we may think that hours of clock time have elapsed when in fact only a few minutes have passed. It is the behaviour of our attention that gives us our own private sense of duration. When it is deep, intense, and steady, it gives us an impression of small duration: when it is light and passing rapidly from thought to thought, we have one of long duration. Despite this irregularity, there is still one thing that remains constant, and that is the sense of the direction of the flow. Whatever happens to our sense of duration, under normal conditions we always retain a clear indication of past, present, and future; always, that is, until, as I shall describe later, we escape from duration altogether, and our impressions of past, present and future are united in an expanded existence, in a new awareness. What I have described is the situation that anyone would find himself in if he were left for a long time without any outside indications of duration. Our inherent time sense, which is one rather of duration only, exists; but it is by clock standards unreliable, though it may be that our own personal standards are really of far more value to us as indicating the rate at which we are experiencing, and therefore living.

How lamentably a clock measures a long moment of intense emotion! Of what real value is it to us to say that it lasted two minutes? It may have represented, perhaps, one hundredth of all our living experience. Some ghastly ten minutes of suffering may have aged us ten years; that is, it may have been the equivalent of ten years' life experience. We are unfortunately rather hypnotized by clock time, which is purely and entirely a convenience, an academic abstraction, and of no real value, without some sort of coefficient of intensity to give it a personal significance: it is also, at times, extremely irksome when it clashes inconveniently with our personal sense of duration.

This sense which we have of our own personal fourth dimension is therefore of much more significance to us than that given by the clock. Our extension in time or duration must be for each one of us a personal one: we do not need a clock to give us this, we provide it for ourselves. As far as our life's experience is concerned, what our minds tell us about the rate at which we are existing is right; it is not irregular; it is clock time that is not true to the varying intensity at which we live and which is therefore unreliable.

Before we are led any further in this direction we must pause for a moment to consider a complication we have introduced by approaching time from these two distinct points of view. We have shewn that academically both the stone and the human being are four-dimensional, but whereas we have an awareness of what this fourth dimension is, the stone can have none. It is we who have thrust this extra dimension on the unsuspecting stone in order that our conception of existence may be satisfied. But if time is to be a fourth dimension, it must be the same for all; it must be as universal as the other three. It must be as real for the stone as it is for us. This is a real puzzler, for our considerations so far have led us to the point where time for us is something quite different to the time dimension we have given the stone. This is the contradiction that we must now resolve.

We can, if we like, look on our sense of duration as the thing about us that prevents us from being static; because of this we know that we are not just 'being', but 'becoming'. And what about the stone? Is it static, or is it also 'becoming'? 'Certainly' we would reply if we were asked, feeling somewhat condescending in answering at all such a stupid question, 'if it can be considered as "becoming" at all, it could not be in the same way that we are.' That, however, would not matter, if we could legitimately consider the stone as 'becoming' in principle, and as having in an unimaginably low degree a sense of duration, the disparity between its fourth dimension and ours would have disappeared. The trouble is that there are two very different conceptions of the type of thing a stone is. We imagine it as a dead, static substance; but the scientist sees it as a turbulent mass of activity, of atoms, and particles of very great variety, all moving in an organized or predictable manner with tremendous energy. He would certainly not consider it as either dead or static. We accept the whole stone as it appears to our eyes, and in this guise its changes are more sedate than those we suffer: but the changes that are actually occurring are in fact far more violent than our mild activities ever are AS AN ORGANIZED BEING of a higher order. But the stone is not this: it is not organized as what we like to call a stone, it is only organized on a much lower and more local scale. As a stone, it is not a 'whole' as a human being is; we must therefore look lower in the scale of organization to see whether there could be anything that corresponds to our time sense. These atomic activities that are occurring on a minute scale must themselves have duration, and we must conclude that on an equally small scale the force (call it electronic, or magnetic, or atomic, or life force,) that is producing and controlling these activities, must possess in its own form what corresponds to an awareness of the duration of its activities. This must be so, otherwise atomic activity would be entirely random, or it would be controlled from 'outside'. And this 'outside' would have to be somewhere higher up the scale of organization, because if it were not we should have to look deeper into the atom for it and it would not then be 'outside'. While there is evidence that the atomic activities are at least not random, there is no evidence that control of their activities exists higher up the organizational scale, for instance in the molecule. It is convenient to accept that atomic activity contains within itself the controlling force, and that implies a primitive sense of duration or awareness of its own fourth dimension. The alternative would make the stone a true three-dimensional body in a universe filled with four-dimensional beings who in order to legitimize its unfortunate position had endowed it with an *ersatz* fourth dimension. But if all creation is one, it must be homogeneous, and the alternative can therefore be ruled out. Some sort of explanation as the one I have given must therefore be the true description of the stone as a four-dimensional thing.

All creation therefore at some level of organization has a knowledge or awareness of itself as a four-dimensional being or thing. But we humans can go further than this, as I shall explain later. We also have the ability to develop an awareness in which the sense of time or duration has ceased to exist—the 'timeless moment' of the mystics, and where therefore we must have achieved an awareness of a fifth dimension of existence. In this awareness, time is no longer sensed, but given, and what is now sensed is a new extension of existence that must remain unimaginable to those who have not experienced it; for it cannot be described except by poetic allegory, because such a new awareness cannot be explained in words that have been made to fit the old.

Our application of attention has two characteristics, depth or intensity, and its rate of change from one thought to another. These characteristics are normally linked; that is to say when attention is light its rate of change is high; and when it is intense its rate is slower. But it is possible by training, and within limits, to deepen attention and maintain its rate of change more or less. This point is however not significant and I shall not take it into account further. When attention is intensified, all the impressions our senses are sending us carry far greater significance. We find that the simplest object is filled with rare beauty and meaning, and is much more of a 'thing' than we had ever believed. Its association with us is much closer and more intimate and has a quality of being mellowed by time. We have been able to read recently quite a lot about the sensation of heightened awareness that results from taking certain drugs, amongst others mescalin; and Mr. Aldous Huxley describes the enriched significance he found in the ordinary things he saw and touched. In these cases, the normal depth or intensity and rate of attention of the drug-takers has been temporarily affected, and a new *constant* level of attention has been introduced. As Mr. Huxley tells us, it not only completely changed the environment reported to him by his senses, but upset his time sense. He was experiencing deeply things that normally hardly roused a flicker of interest, and the minutes that slipped away while he contemplated the shade of a flower or the texture of the material of his suit passed unnoticed. Drugs will presumably be found that will do the opposite, that is, increase the speed with which the attention passes from thought to thought and give the drug-taker the impression of living an hour in the space of a few clock minutes. What is interesting about these experiments, apart from the novelty of the sense impressions, is that the drug, presumably by chemical action, shifts the level of stability about which attention normally only varies slightly, and enables it to stabilize itself at this new level.

We might wonder why attention should stabilize itself at any level. Why does it always tend to come back to what we experience as its normal depth and rate? Should it not be possible to alter the intensity and speed with which we perceive things at will? What is it that makes such a condition unstable? I have found some help in this problem in a remarkable book by the Frenchman Pierre Latil which has been translated by Golla and which in the English translation is called *Thinking by Machine*. What becomes apparent in designing a machine with the degree of self-organization that is now possible, is that the rate at which it surveys its environment with whatever instruments it has been given for this purpose must be fixed within fairly narrow limits, in order that the machine shall be able to adapt itself to the environment in which it is to exist. And the rate must be fixed, so that the motor effects, that is, the limbs, etc., have time to be put into action before the next message from the sensing instruments is received to cancel or alter them. If insufficient time is allowed in the setting of the machine it will exist in a continual state of stuttering and nothing will be achieved. This rate of reception of sense data could be described as a sort of 'brain rhythm' and it must be maintained by the internal mechanism of the machine within fairly close limits. This 'brain rhythm' would seem to be directly applicable to the attention of the human being. Our normal depth and rate of attention is that to which we have organized ourselves through the necessity of being able to exist in our environment. A lesser degree of attention to the mass of sense impressions that crowd in on us continually during our waking hours would mean that essentials for our self-preservation would be missed, and we should suffer accordingly. A greater degree of attention would of course mean the same thing. We should find ourselves concentrating on insignificant details, as far as our self-preservation was concerned, but these details would fill our whole being with a sense of completion, meanwhile, not having reacted to the horn, we should be run over by the motor-car. Our attention must be just so finely adjusted to the impressions we constantly receive from our environment that it will not only not be tempted to dwell on the unnecessary ones, but will shift at a speed suited to our muscular response. We can of course by drugs or by other means artificially alter either the things that carry significance, or the behaviour of our attention, but we must in that case alter as well our mode of existence. And if we wish to develop an increased awareness, brought about by heightened attention, we must follow the sort of existence that will allow this to happen. Hence the rigorous routine of the Satipatthana course. A shift in degree of attention necessarily alters our time sense: it would be reasonable to imagine that too great a speeding up would result in the complete breakdown of the individual, but at the other extreme there would be no such danger, and it is in fact here where a startling expansion of the individual can occur.

If we want to shift the centre about which our attention finds its equilibrium, we need something more than just an effort of will, however strong this may be. We need to alter the control which normally steps in and brings it back, when it tends to get too far away from what is necessary to allow us to remain adapted to our environment. It has been demonstrated that this can be done by drugs, but these experiments have also made it clear that if we were to live permanently in this state we should soon be shut away as a danger to ourselves and to others. It can also be done by progressive exercises in concentration and contemplation. In the day-long contemplation on the body and the mind that is the aim of the Satipatthana training, there is a definite increase in the depth of attention held by the will. It is however very slight, not to be compared with the change that takes place as the result of taking mescalin. In the state of complete 'mindfulness', that is when the mind in unwaveringly following the activities of the body, and when necessary the moods of the mind, there is, as I have already stated in an earlier chapter, a slowing up of all one's movements, which take on a curiously deliberate, sleep-walking pattern. The reason for this can now be well understood. All activities must be adapted to the new relationship to the environment caused by the change in the depth and rate of attention. And when contemplation of this sort is complete there is no appreciation of any slowing up. It may well be possible to break the apparent linkage between depth and rate so that a man who possessed a deeper degree of attention could live in the same environment as anyone else; but he would not be considered normal, as his reactions to everything perceived by his senses would be so very different to ours. It would also, one imagines, put such a strain on his mechanism for selecting which impressions to act on, and which to ignore, that the resulting unaccountable behaviour would inevitably end in breakdown.

We can readily understand therefore why we have a fairly constant depth and rate of attention, and what purpose this serves. We shall consider now what happens when we try to develop control of attention so that it can become deeper and unwavering. What we have discussed so far has shewn that it is the wavering of the attention that gives us a sense of time, so that if our contemplation is not absolutely steady we shall still possess such a sense, though by clock time it will be completely 'haywire'. In deep contemplation we have put ourselves into the situation of the man in the dark room, since we have excluded all messages from our senses and are quite unaware of our physical surroundings. In the Satipatthana exercises, it will be remembered that one is continually following up the wandering attention, and bringing it back to the subject of contemplation, and that this process is continued without relaxation until the attention can be held absolutely steady. When this happens and the practice is continued further, the object of contemplation itself will fade away and the attention will still be held rock steady, with no thought content at all. This is what the Buddhists call 'formless contemplation'. But even in contemplation with form, that is when there is still thought content before the attention, the sense of time will be entirely eliminated. The flow will have stopped; there will be no past, present, and future. Our own personal clock has run down, and time as an awareness for us has ceased to exist.

It is this stage that I believe the Buddhists interpret by the phrase 'the attainment of cessation' which occurs in their scriptures without much explanation of what it means. There also occur references to 'planes of time' which I have found difficult to place in the understanding of time that I have been describing. During the Satipatthana training, there were, for me anyhow, no quantum jumps in the time sense; there were no definite steps corresponding to a particular change in the depth and rate of attention. But that is not to say that such steps do not exist, and that there may well be levels of organization that have their own time sense that differs from ours in just this very quality. To revert to the stone, it is reasonable to suppose that at the level of atomic activity, which is the level at which we were prepared to accept the stone as a four-dimensional thing, the time sense of the controlling element would have to be something that worked a shade faster than ours. In fact the attention of whatever controls the movements of these very small particles would have to be lighter and quicker to a degree that we can hardly imagine. This time sense could be described as a 'plane of time'; and there may well be others both relatively deeper and lighter than ours that belong to organizations higher and lower than that in which we exist.

If we persist with the deep contemplation 'with form' until the subject of contemplation has itself faded away, we shall then pass into 'contemplation without form'. There are many descriptions of this experience, none of which can give it substance to one who has not experienced it. It is the 'timeless moment' of the mystics. The immense expansion of consciousness that takes place has been likened to absorbing the whole of creation, and of entering into an existence in a completely different sphere, or in many spheres or planes. However those who have experienced it try to describe or explain it, it remains meaningless to us, except as a very vague exalted state; and it leaves some sceptical, others envious. The sense of time has been completely left behind and what masqueraded as such is now a given fact of our previous commonplace existence. It could not be sensed any more, for the attention that gave us the sense is stilled. But instead there is a new awareness, an overwhelming sense of expansion into an existence in many new planes simultaneously, and an extraordinary extension of comprehension. All that before was inexplicable is now simple. This new awareness, as do all awarenesses, opens up a whole world of new experiences. We would seem to be existing in a new dimension—a fifth dimension, and it could well be defined as being at right angles to what we knew as time.

And so we are back where we started. The real puzzle is not time, but dimensions. The bare matter-of-factness of dimensions as we have been taught to understand them has led us astray. I do not think it helps to consider them from the point of view of either the mathematician or the scientist. I remember reading in a scientific work that in reality there are in the universe twelve dimensions, but at any one time six of them are always equal to zero. Such a statement, I would think, became necessary in order to explain some complicated formula which had collected too many terms in its development. It may have meant something to him; it may even be true. But it can mean nothing to you and me, and I would say that if any of it is true, the last part of the statement certainly is not. A dimension should mean something, if it is in fact a thing that helps to measure and encompass our existence.

The deduction that must now be clear from all I have said about time is that a dimension is nothing more or less than a field of awareness, a field of experiencing. Starting from the point, which represents bare awareness with no content, through the next three dimensions with gradually developing awareness, we arrive at our present normal full experience as a four-dimensional being. But this does not end the story. As a being whose prospect is to reveal in its fullness the spirit which our material existence is mostly hiding, we must continue to find new awarenesses until we reach that of ultimate life force, spirit, God, or Nibbana; and individuality disappears. How many dimensions we shall discover *en route* is an intriguing thought; it may well be the twelve of the scientist, but if so, they will all be equal to *something* all the time.

We need not therefore be deterred by a fifth dimension. It is merely the next extension of experience. It will be, as time is to us, unmeasurable; and it will contain within itself a whole new content of knowledge. Nobody who has experienced it has to the best of my knowledge ever said so, but I believe if it were possible while in this awareness to look back and see what our time looks like, it would appear as a clear measurement, a clear extension neither clocked, nor linked to attention. It would be something that could be conceived as a whole, not as a flow, in the same way as we now think of length, breadth and thickness.

I have no doubt that this awareness of a fifth extension exists in embryo in every human being but that the vehicle for its expression requires careful preparation. Taking drugs is no short cut, though we may in this way find experiences that lie on the way. The secret lies in learning to control attention, and this can only be done by some such training as Satipatthana. The discoveries that the mind will make in the new awareness will remain uninterpretable because there are no words to convey the meaning that the experience holds; and on returning to a four-dimensional existence the clarity of the new knowledge will fade, just as our dream does on waking, and for the same reason. Only where it affects directly the problems of existence in time, will certainty have been brought back; and in some cases, questions we regard as insoluble will be resolved in the afterglow of the new awareness.

9

DISTRACTIONS

STRANGELY enough I did not feel tempted to work out in my mind the matters I have dealt with in the last two chapters. I adopted the attitude of Scarlet O'Hara, 'I won't think about that today, I'll think about it tomorrow,' and opportunity to do this came later during my long voyage back to England from Singapore. Each time that I got up from the floor of the Sayadaw's house or from under the fan in the lecture hall, collected my sandals and started on my way back to my cell block, the matters that had been discussed faded, and my mind once more settled down to the 'lift, swing, down', of the hot walk back.

I had, after the strangeness of the first few days had worn off, very soon adapted myself to the quiet uneventful routine, and in fact resented interruptions. The news must have got round that there was an Englishman here doing the course because quite a number of Indians and Burmese came to see me and most enthusiastically wished me success with my meditations. They were mostly laymen who had at some time done the course and were returning either for a 'refresher' or to visit their friends among the monks. Although I was flattered by their attention, I did not like being jerked out of my strict meditation routine (for any excuse to break it made it more difficult to take up again); but I had some very interesting conversations with my visitors. I came to believe that meditation with the Burmese was as common a subject for conversation as the weather in England! The retiring Commissioner of Police, who had already done the course twice and was a frequent visitor, told me that many government servants do it, and return from time to time for periods of intense meditation. The greeting of all who came to see me was always accompanied by 'And how is your meditation progressing?' and real interest was shewn in the stage I had reached and any difficulties I was having. It was comforting to know that many people leading the sort of life that I had been living, and with no particular mystic leanings, had successfully got through the course and derived benefit from it.

I was in no doubt that meditation in Burma was more generally and more sincerely practised than prayer in most Christian countries. Most of the educated people, in their desire to undergo a period of strict meditation were prompted, I think, by a genuine wish to press on with their development as the Buddha had instructed them to do. But I observed one afternoon towards the end of my time a group of very old people who were waiting to enter the Sayadaw's house. They were a motley collection who must have been very near life's end; and they looked very poor and very wretched. I asked U Pe Thin about them. He told me that the Sayadaw held regular classes of instruction for old people who wished to be taught meditation in order to avoid being sent back to this world again. I could not help but think that they had left it rather late, and that this sort of deathbed conversion could be of little value to a Buddhist, who should believe that what he was trying to avoid was the very thing he needed and had unfortunately neglected to take advantage of. Presumably they had been followers of the ritual of their faith without putting much effort into the hard work of real meditation. Now they realized that their life had been far from enjoyable and that it was worth while taking the pains they had up to now omitted to take, to avoid having to return to the earth again to suffer the same hardships. They were sitting patiently in the hot sun outside, this ragged group of both men and women; and I watched them troop in as I went out, feeling almost a partaker in this deception as they prostrated themselves eagerly, and then sat waiting for the miracle to happen that would relieve them of the awful prospect of return. We were in the same boat, these old ones and I: we were both seeking the same thing, but I was not driven, as they were, by the fear of returning to the scene of their present discomfort. I had been luckier—this time! They came once a week, U Pe Thin told me, but he could hold out little hope for them, except that their efforts would comfort their dying days, and might start them off with a better chance next time.

Fortunately the interruptions after the first week became fewer and fewer. I think it became known that I was not just a curious visitor, but a serious meditator, and my need for privacy was respected. But there were times during the following weeks when I found the need for a break too strong to resist, and because by then the stream of visitors had dried up I arranged some minor distraction, like a walk to the huge reclining statue of the Buddha, that was a frequently visited shrine only a little way outside the

Centre. But there was one event that happened about a week before I left that was particularly welcome. I had reached a point where the sitting-walking-sitting routine seemed to stretch endlessly into the future, and I was making very little apparent progress. In this case, U Pe Thin told me about it and suggested I should take part. There was to be an important celebration in the big lecture hall to honour five monks who had achieved notable success in their studies. It was to be a day of festival; there would be stalls and decorations; the Prime Minister and other government officials with all the notables of the town would attend, and the ceremony would be preceded by a feast in the library opposite. I thought that in any case my daily examination would be off, and there would probably be a good deal of disturbance throughout the Centre, as a great number of the public would be allowed in, so that I would lose little by attending. It would be an interesting spectacle, though I was warned that it would consist mostly of speeches, and I would of course understand nothing. I was in some doubt as to how I should be dressed. Everybody would be in their best clothes, silk longyis and jackets for the men, blouses or jackets for the women. U Pe Thin suggested trousers and a shirt but I felt that would make me much too conspicuous, and I decided in favour of a longyi and the quietest of my cotton sports shirts. Even so my very dowdiness amongst so much finery would be bound to attract attention.

A day or so before the celebration was due to take place there were great preparations both inside the hall and outside on the wide roadway where the stalls and decorations were to be set up. Such peace as the crows, the dogs, and the bells left to us was given up to an air of excitement and expectation that affected even the monks in my block, and they gathered in small groups before they went off in the morning on their forage for food. I had often wondered about their food collecting and would have liked to have accompanied one of them on the morning tour, but did not like to ask. They went off armed with their large lacquer bowls with smaller containers inside for the spices, meat and odd vegetables they ate with their rice; and they came back about an hour later loaded with enough food to feed half a dozen men. The surplus rice was fed to the dogs and the crows and this was the only food the dogs had. I wondered how they always managed to return with such overflowing bowls, and always at exactly the same time, and I asked my friend the milkman who had a cell in my block how the system worked. He told me that they all had their own special houses that undertook to provide and cook their morning meal for them, some perhaps had two or three; even the poorest people were glad to contribute what they could, and a monk never had any difficulty in getting all he needed.

Even my cell block, which was some distance from the hall, was drawn into the new activities, and the comings and goings of cars, each leaving a swirl of dust to settle hesitantly with our regained peace, forced me to keep my windows shut and to find new places for walking.

Very early on the day, as soon as it was light, the stalls filled up with a great assortment of goods. Cloths and silks of all descriptions, books, sweetmeats and highly coloured fruit drinks in large glass jars, looking like the great jars of coloured liquids one sees in old-fashioned chemist shops. Each stall was decorated with paper pennants that were gay in the breeze that sprang up towards the end of the day, but in the morning still and dignified to match the solemnity of the occasion. Just behind the library where the feast was taking place tables were set up with more food and drink for those who were allowed to eat later in the day. The programme had been arranged so that the eating would all be over in time for the ceremony to start at eleven-thirty. Although I had been invited to eat with the rest in the library, I decided not to, as I knew they would have far more than I could manage, and I did not want to appear unappreciative of their food.

U Pe Thin had given me the previous day a brief description of what would be happening and what it was all about. The five monks who were to be honoured had achieved special distinction in an examination, by reciting a major portion of the Buddhist scriptures by heart. The particular books they had learnt added up to some thousand pages. This feat of memory is tested by an examination that lasts forty-five days, during which isolated pages picked at random by five judges are recited until each book has been dealt with in full. This oral examination is followed by a written one on the subject and meaning of the texts. There is one monk, whose photograph was exhibited in the hall on this occasion, who must possess a phenomenal memory, for he can recite the whole twelve thousand pages of the Buddhist scriptures. I believe this feat has only once before been equalled in Buddhist history, and that a very long time ago. What useful purpose such feats serve is hard to understand, but that they were held in very great esteem was clear from the scale of the affair and the attendance of the highest in the land at the celebration. Each monk was presented with a little wooden box containing a scroll and some other object which I could not identify; and a silk flag in a little golden cylinder which I learnt would be flown from the bonnet of any car they might be travelling in (just as I did in Singapore, but without first having to acquire the tremendous mental qualification of the monks!). I could only imagine that this was a tradition handed down from the times when the scriptures were not recorded, and it was by similar feats of memory that the teaching was passed from monk to monk. I could admire this phenomenal ability, but I could not help feeling that there were better ways of using such talent.

I arrived at the hall early, at least three-quarters of an hour before the proceedings were due to start, and carrying my sandals in with me I squatted down at the back of the hall where the less well dressed seemed to be sitting. But presently a friend came along and asked me to move, as I was sitting in the area reserved for ladies! I was then led up to a row about six from the front, where the contrast I had avoided brought me many curious glances, and I must have looked like a beggar in a Chinese play. All around me were men in beautiful silk longyis and elaborately worked silk or satin jackets. I was, too, the only hatless one in a sea of elegant silk hats, the colours of which obviously held some social distinction. They consisted of small squat fez-shaped basketwork forms, covered in pink, yellow, or white silk, tied in a floppy bow over the right ear. We sat close together on bright red and yellow mats which had been unrolled over the whole floor. I hoped sincerely that my dowdy appearance wouldn't give the impression that I was not treating this celebration with proper respect.

In front of us were five separate thrones for the monks who were to be honoured; each consisted of a dais covered in rich yellow silk on which was placed a large orange cushion. These thrones were each flanked by two ornate pagoda-shaped umbrellas of white silk with gold edgings and dangling leaves of gold. Presently the five monks came in, climbed on to their thrones and sat down gracefully on their cushions. Here they were to sit immovable with downcast eyes for the two and a half hours of the ceremony, except for one of them, whose dark flashing eyes darted here and there, either through curiosity or excitement. He was younger than the rest, and his interest in the audience was in such sharp contrast to the passive immobility of the others that it drew my attention like a lighthouse on a dark coast. Three of the other monks were not marked by any distinction: their orange robes and shaven heads were common to the couple of hundred other monks who were present, and only served to emphasize their impersonality. They were symbols of human striving not personal achievement; and their massive immobility was a gesture that acknowledged without accepting any personal share in the honour that was being paid them. But the one on my left, who looked older than the others, had a gaunt, fixed look that might well have been the result of his recent efforts. It fell to him to recite the passages that were repeated by the whole assembly before the speeches began. But some of them he said alone; they were very long, and were delivered without pause, as though he wished to avoid any inference by the audience that he, who was being honoured for reciting one thousand pages, was unable to deal with this comparatively short recitation without stopping to think what came next! The Buddhist 'prayers', or repetitions of the scriptures as most of them are, are usually spoken in a curiously monotonous nasal tone, and always as though they were something to be got over as quickly as possible, without any suggestion of a personal rendering lending emphasis or conviction to the bare words. This monk got through his task at a rattling good speed, and the pauses he was forced to make for breath were accompanied by a convulsive gulping swallow which served at the same time to clear his throat, and for which he appeared to grudge even the half second or so he allowed for it. I was so fascinated in watching his delivery, that I found myself omitting to follow the hand and head actions with which my fellow squatters were punctuating his words.

Just before the ceremony began, and the last to enter the hall, a number of old Sayadaws, who had presumably retired from active administrative work, filed in and took their seats facing the audience behind the five monks. I noticed Mahasi among them, and I spent some time studying the faces of these men who had lived lives of rigid self-discipline and constant meditation. What would I expect to find in them? How would passionless experience leave its mark? Even amongst the strong, serene faces I had become used to they were remarkable. One or two were very old, but their faces still held the deep confidence that spoke of a life of unwavering dedicated purpose, not in conflict and strife and self-denigration, but in satisfaction and success. There were many different types, but each had a compelling characteristic that brought my attention back again and again during the long speeches. The similarity between them and the faces of a group of retired senior officers of the fighting services was so strong that I could almost imagine there were some I knew amongst them, dressed rather incongruously in orange robes! They all had that far-away look in their eyes that Noel Coward once so bitingly remarked was supposed to be the result of scanning the distant horizon, but in the Naval Officer actually came from drinking too much gin. (In all fairness to him, I must record that during a subsequent visit to the fleet at sea, he withdrew the remark and said he thought there was something in the horizon business after all.) These were faces of men of deep experience who had spent their lives searching for knowledge within themselves, without looking for help from a God of any sort. They had been, and still were, 'working out their salvation with diligence' as instructed by the Buddha, and in doing so had acquired an understanding of the strength and frailty of human beings. Similarly, however, did not go further than their faces, for all these old Sayadaws were sitting as few admirals or generals could, with their legs tucked under them on the hard wooden armchairs that must have made it a doubly difficult and uncomfortable position, and their feet were twisted in behind the arm supports.

At the beginning of each new speech, I found considerable interest in the way it was being delivered, but as it continued and I could get no hint of what it was about, my attention returned to the Sayadaws, and I saw the faces of the picture gallery at the Royal Naval College at Greenwich, and in other places where the well-known fighting personalities of Hitler's war were hung for posterity. Here was a startling link between two very different ways of occupying one's energies, and an indication that all discipline to be effective must begin with self-discipline, and that responsibility brings with it a greater need for this and not a lesser as those in the lower ranks so often imagine. These old monks, like my associates, had first been taught discipline and then found the need for the support of self-discipline in the living of their very different lives.

The ceremony began with the recitations led by the eager monk; then followed speeches read or intoned from a lectern placed centrally in front of the five monks. To me, not understanding any Burmese, these speeches were tedious and unnoteworthy, with the exception of one or two very curious intonations that must have been specially acquired for occasions of this sort. They were really chants without tune but with a quick and surprisingly varied intonation. Each phrase ended in the same way in an upward accented twiddle that I had to be careful not to laugh at, but which I found extremely comic and unexpected in such a solemn and dignified proceeding. These chanters relieved the monotony of what must, I think, have been for all, too many speeches. They were, after all, congratulating five monks on learning one thousand pages off by heart, and two hours is a long time in which to do that.

As each speech ended, I hoped it would be the last, and eventually this was so, and instead of anybody else getting up to go to the lectern, a girls' choir, seated on the opposite side of the hall to me, started to sing. I had noticed these girls as I came in, and wondered if they were taking part in the ceremony. They were young, with the typical wide-eyed round face of the Burmese, and were dressed alike in thin white blouses and purple longyis. And they all wore flowers in their hair. They sang sitting down in the customary nasal voices that for me held little musical quality; but their song was melodious and rhythmic, and in fact quite a catchy little tune. The girls looked fresh and charming and their turn was a most welcome relief after the interminable speeches. I was a little surprised when they began, however, as one of the precepts I and all the monks, and presumably many others, had taken was not to sing or

dance, and here was temptation laid on in a very alluring
way! The tune remained in my mind, and when I got back
to my cell I hastily scribbled it down. But unfortunately the
paper got lost, and the tune with it.

After the singing the ceremony suddenly ended. The
monks filed out and we got up stiffly from the floor. A few
groups remained chatting in the comparative cool of the
hall; the rest flocked out either to wander round the stalls,
or those who were allowed to eat after midday to the tables
loaded with rice and meat dishes, fruit and drink, standing
in the sparse shade of the few trees that still retained their
leaves. For a moment I regretted the restriction I was under,
but it was anyhow too hot outside, and I turned my steps
towards the track that led back to my cell block—'lift,
swing, down; lift, swing, down'. The bustling crowds
receded: silk hats, round faces, speeches and monks faded
like a dream too lightly constructed for the awakened
sensibilities; but in this case it was being pushed out of
reach of the attention, and the simple activities of my
existence began once again to fill my horizon.

My last week at the Centre was a really critical time.
U Pe Thin spent much of it trying to persuade me that I was
just on the point of achieving 'samadhi', the state of fixed
attention in deep concentration, and that all I had to do was
to persevere without impatience and without desire for
achievement. This was of course difficult, and while I felt
myself that limited success was not far off, I felt equally
that I might require another two or three weeks to still my
attention finally into submission. There was, to make these
days more difficult, a disturbing influence in our block. A
young man, the owner of a chain of sterilized milk factories,
had recently arrived for a refresher course in Satipatthana.

I never discovered whether he was really serious about it or whether he was here to avoid some unpleasant business complication or perhaps even to qualify for a reduction of taxes! He brought with him a good deal of miscellaneous gear including a deck-chair, and on several occasions when passing his cell, I noticed him stretched out apparently asleep in it. Of course he may have been meditating. It was difficult to say! He had a servant who attended him; called him in the morning about six with tea, and later brought his breakfast, cleaned his room (and incidentally pinched my broom to do it! Each cell had its own cleaning devices hanging up outside, and for a while I had to borrow until I think one of the monks put the matter right). The milkman spent a lot of time talking to anybody he could persuade to join him on the verandah, and always in a loud voice; so that competition for 'walking' in the back verandah became intense. He spoke good English, but after a few polite words when he first arrived, I kept out of his way. His wife and children arrived every day in a flurry of dust, and she stayed talking with him in his cell while the children played outside. Altogether he caused a lot of disturbance to our unvarying routine and I seriously considered asking to be moved elsewhere. But as it happened he turned out to be a good friend in need when the water famine struck us. Without warning, our water just stopped running and there was no other source from where we could fetch it. The small lake where I stopped each morning had by now been reduced to a shallow pond, and the water was very dirty. All the other cell blocks were in the same predicament. When this had been going on for some forty-eight hours, I was preparing to get in touch with the Buddhist Council Headquarters to fetch me for a clean-up in the town. It was at this point that the milkman offered to drive me to his house for a bath, an offer I quickly accepted. And when the car arrived that morning with his wife, I hopped in and was taken, not to his house, but to one of his factories a few miles down the road which he said would be more satisfactory. There was, he added, an excellent shower that he had had specially fitted in one of the office blocks. It was there all right, but had obviously been used for refuse of every sort and smelt to high heaven. However, one of the men set to and removed as much of the dirt as he could and after some persuasion got it to function. With some diffidence I had my shower and finished up feeling a little cleaner. Afterwards I was given a most refreshing glass of his milk, the product of the factory, and just managed to get it down before midday when milk came under the ban. I was very grateful to the milkman for this interlude: he must have guessed my discomfort because no one else seemed to worry about the situation, and I don't know how they managed. Fortunately the situation improved the next day when we had water for a couple of hours and were able to fill our hundred-gallon drum. The milkman continued with his disturbing habits, but I was able to regard them in a more charitable light, and managed to avoid the worst and overcome the effect of the rest.

The limited success in my meditation that was all I knew I could expect came almost unperceived and at a time when I seemed to be having the usual occasional distracting thought. One minute I was still recalling my attention from its wandering with the patience that what felt like long habit had bred, and the next minute I realized after a period that was neither long nor short, that it had at last ceased to stray and had been held effortlessly steady. It was as easy and simple as that. There was no sudden deep extasy or any certainty of the birth of a new experience. It was just that stillness had intervened and the battle with the constantly shifting attention was won. But it was only just in time. I forget now whether it was two or three days before I had my last interview and said 'goodbye' to the two Sayadaws, Mahasi and Shwesedi, but it seemed a very short time. My farewells were brief: Mahasi gave me some advice on continuing the practices when I had returned to an active life. Shwesedi took me to his temporary quarters under the small lecture hall and produced a snapshot of himself in meditation posture (all photographs in the Centre were taken in this position, and I was myself photographed by the Centre's amateur photographer before I left). He took a piece of headed paper of his Monastery in Mandalay and wrote on it laboriously in English 'When you write you can send your letter to this address.' Then as I thanked him he looked up and said in short, clipped words, 'And you will write every week?' I said no, not every week, but I would certainly write, and hoped he would be able to understand my English. I hoped, too, that it would be possible for me to return to Burma sometime to finish the course with him at Mandalay.

My plane was due out from Rangoon about 1.45 a.m. and I was being fetched some three-quarters of an hour before that by one of the Council representatives. I spent much of the last evening in a long conversation with the milkman, leaning over the concrete balustrade of the verandah outside my cell. It was about midnight and as usual there were a couple of monks walking up and down, either in the moonlight or at the other end of the block. It was unusual for the milkman to be up at this time, but he was restless, and, I think, lonely; his time was nearly up and I was one of the many brooms he used to sweep his loneliness away. It was a lovely, clear, still moonlit night; and for once the dogs were quiet though I knew this would not last. They howled in unison at fairly regular intervals every night, and when the moon was up these intervals were more frequent. I had a feeling that I was on the eve of a great adventure, returning to the busy world again; and I was a little apprehensive. Restriction always brings with it an added sense of security, and even though the restriction under which I had been living was a mental one, and might be considered for that reason easy to lift, it had been more real and compelling than any I had previously experienced. All my problems during the last three weeks or so had been highly localized and intimate ones, and I had been shut away from the many influences that normally form part of our daily experience wherever we are. Here, looking through the bare trees at the scene given such clarity by the moonlight, where everything appears to be either light or dark, either yes or no, and where no difficult inbetweens exist, I felt strangely incompetent to deal with the expansion of experience that I must face tomorrow.

We talked of Burma, of his milk business, of the Satipatthana training, and of things I have referred to earlier on. But he had been silent for some minutes and I did not wish to break the intimate familiarity of the scene that was part of this experience that had bitten so deeply into me, and which I wanted to remember as it was, without the frills that memory so easily adds; a picture that was almost arid in its simplicity and in a way, I felt, representative of the last three weeks.

'Will you come back to Burma?'

I thought he would ask me that, and I did not know how to answer. Apart from a wish to be polite, I had no feeling about it.

'This sort of thing is easy for you,' I replied, 'it is part of your accepted life: you don't have to fit it in: you don't even have to question it to see whether it produces something you can live with. You know it does. I must have time to digest what I have discovered here, to see what part it can play in my life; whether it will enrich my experience outside the Centre or merely complicate it. And if it enriches it, how I shall want to make use of the changed significance I shall then find in the things I do and the people I live with. When I have answered these questions I shall know whether I shall want to return to Burma and continue the process. At the moment, of course, I feel I would like to have had the time to finish the course, to find out what is to be gained from the insight that I am now so sure would come with further practice. As it is I can't. And I have always believed in taking time to digest new ideas, so perhaps it is just as well. I need that time now, and I know that the process cannot be hurried.'

'I think you will come again,' he said. 'We would like to feel that we have given you something you value enough to make you want to come back for more.'

He spoke as so many others had spoken whom I had seen in the last day or so; U Pe Thin, my friend who gave me my daily meal, the members of the Council who had made the arrangements for my departure. All hoped I had found the course valuable and had derived permanent benefit from it. They had personal experience of its value, and wished that I too should share it.

Presently the peace was broken. I heard the car turn in

at the gates of the Centre. The dogs heard it too and pandemonium started up. I went back to my cell to collect my case and to look for the last time at the bare walls that had contained my hours of effort. I had no personal feeling for it, for most of my existence had been spent behind my closed eyes. But the mosquitoes should welcome my departure!

I shook hands with the milkman, and wished him luck with his meditation. The driver looked surly and obviously wasn't even going to open the door for me. Why do aeroplanes always seem to leave at the most inconvenient hours? I got in and we turned and drove slowly through the settling dust, down the track, past the Sayadaw's house, the lecture hall, and out through the gates with their *papier-mâché* dragons into the familiar and yet unfamiliar world.

AFTERMATH

As the familiar world engulfed me once more, many of the adjustments that were necessary were automatic and unconscious; but some weren't. I found that I was more deliberately conscious of the less significant things that went on around me, that I seemed to be manipulating my mind like a searchlight to focus on everything that came to my attention. But gradually this sensation left me and I returned to the normal routine in which the mind records little of what the senses report. I was pretty busy on my return, mainly with social activities, and for a time I certainly felt far more power behind my mind whenever I had to use it, which wasn't really very often! But this too gradually faded, whether through becoming accustomed to its more efficient functioning, or because I lost the skill I had acquired I don't know: probably it was for both reasons; but I was led to believe that I had gained no permanent advantage from my efforts. It was difficult at that time to sum up my impressions of the visit and the course, because there was too much going on, and most of my immediate impressions were physical. I had lost more than a stone and a half in weight (which I could well afford to lose)! I required less to eat than before, which was a new difficulty where every social activity requires one either to eat or drink or both; and I needed less sleep. This latter result was a distinct advantage in an occupation where it was difficult to get more than five hours' sleep a night, although one sometimes spent rather longer in bed. These immediate physical results were the main ones I had to contend with: any deeper effects I was content to leave on one side to become apparent in their own time when the process of digestion had been completed. I did, however, manage to continue the sitting practice by getting up half an hour or so earlier each morning, and I was usually up before sunrise; after this it became too hot anyhow to stay in bed. I would not willingly have given up this early-morning practice, for I found it most stimulating and refreshing, and it left me with greater confidence to face the problems of the day.

On the long voyage back to England, at least during the hot weather part of the trip, I had plenty of time to think as I lazed in a deck chair in the sun, or in the shade of the boat deck. But the sun and heat discourage active penetrative thought and are more conducive to a feeling of cosy satisfaction that is entirely sensuous in origin. It is too good, too valuable, and too rare to miss, and although I could have shut myself up in my air-conditioned cabin, I much preferred not to. One criticism I knew I should meet, for I had heard it already, and it seemed to be the first to come into people's minds whenever unusual mental states have been assisted by a rigid dietary routine. 'Don't you think,' I was asked, 'that the effects you thought you were getting from your meditation were really brought about because you were light-headed from too little to eat and lack of sleep?' Because it is indeed possible to induce hallucinations by starving oneself, this is a suggestion that needs answering. The fact is, however, that too little to eat was not a require-ment of the course, merely a reduction of intake of food to what was adequate. The monks ate a lot more than I did. They had, for instance, a large bowl of rice in the mornings with their tea, and another very large bowl with their ten o'clock meal. I found I didn't need it. I am normally a very small eater and the one meal plus the banana or apple that I had with my tea at five-thirty in the morning satisfied me. I was even advised by those who came to see me to take glucose (which for some strange reason was allowed) if I felt weak in the afternoons. But I didn't. No, a state of hypersensitivity through semi-starvation was certainly not encouraged, and the monks all looked sturdy and well fed. I am quite certain that the reduction of food could not possibly have led to any light-headed state; I am also sure that if I had eaten more, or later in the day, I should never have been able to remain awake during the hottest time of the afternoon! As to sleep, the very relaxed state in which one spent the day made more sleep unnecessary. I never had more trouble in getting up than I usually do, and only on a few occasions, when there were good reasons, did I have to break off my practices before midnight and go to bed.

The heightening of the awareness of my sense impres-sions that I have spoken about appeared in retrospect to be most important. I had discovered a value in things that I knew could always be recalled, and there was a deeper sense of the uniqueness of each sound, sight, and touch, that was permanently satisfying. I could now understand what

Powys had been getting at with his 'icthyosaurus ego'—
that part of the human being that gives the primeval response
to the contacts with nature made by our senses. The development of a sensitivity of this sort results in living with
nature and not just as an observer of it, and must in itself
be part of the adjustment I was seeking. I had imagined that
it was only experienced by the artistic and the 'sensitives'.
This alignment of oneself with nature was a soothing
influence that was apparent day and night. It meant that
things had more significance of themselves and less from the
many associations they immediately conjured up. It was an
unexpected gift from Rangoon, this enrichment of reception
that so increased one's joy of perception—a joy without
the exuberance that was usually tied to an anticipation of
some sort. There was no 'How wonderful that will be'
about it, there wasn't even the realization of something that
might be expressed by 'How wonderful it is to be here.'
It was a joy that required nothing but the deep and quiet
satisfaction of being, for instance, part of a sound—those
lovely liquid notes of the oriole, or the rustling of the wind
in the rubber trees that I heard so often in my house. How
often a moment of pure joy is spoilt because someone who
is sharing it feels he must say something about it! There are
so many who feel that appreciation of beauty must immediately be expressed in appreciative words. This feeling of
being part of a thing, a sound, or some lovely scene, is
truer than we usually realize; for in itself the thing does not
exist as such, it is our sense organs, brains and finally our
minds that between them convert the vibrations or the light
waves into the sound or sight that thrills us. The beauty is
our clothing of some prosaic electro-magnetic or other
wave! So we should feel a part of it, and the very fact of

exclaiming over it separates it from us and makes us more of a beholder and less of a sharer of the beauty we have constructed. We are all unconscious artists, we weave the stuff of beauty from the properties and ingredients of matter. A rose is only a rose because man sees it as such; without him it would only be a pattern of energy vortices. Because of this new realization, I took pride in all sorts of beauty that before I had ignored. Sound and sight are purely personal interpretations; we should therefore enjoy as sensually as possible this artistry of our own creation. Unfortunately we are apt to be so proud of the creation of our hands that we miss the far more remarkable continuous creation of our minds.

I found myself often during those pleasant but unfamiliar days at sea (for although my life had been spent at sea, I had never before done a long ocean voyage as a passenger) returning to the quiet meditation that after all the struggle now came so naturally. It was so easy to drop into, a few idle moments were enough to quieten the rhythm of one's being and to bring peace and refreshment. What I found of particular benefit now was the habit I had formed of practising in various positions, standing, sitting on a hard chair, or lying down, as well as in the more usual cross-legged position. It was now possible in any of these positions to feel a familiarity that encouraged the quietening process.

Suez came and went, and it became cooler as we approached Italy. At Genoa, where we stayed forty-eight hours, it was really cold—the first cold I had experienced for two and a half years. In spite of it I ventured ashore; a ship in harbour is a dead thing and passengers a nuisance. Every encouragement in the form of sightseeing tours and excursions was arranged and the passenger lounges were full of men in peaked caps selling the delights of Genoa. But I preferred not to be organized, and sneaked over the gangway with a guilty feeling of playing truant. In the big square, I found a bus going to Portofino for the equivalent of five shillings return, and decided to go along. These buses that career along the riviera coast are expertly handled; and they need to be, for the roads are in places narrow, steep, and twisty; and to add to these natural hazards every other Italian driver seems to be in a hurry for death. There is no speed limit, and although I believe the accident rate is very high, the strange thing is that in a fairly long experience of driving in Italy I have never seen a crash. On this occasion I concluded that there must be a special beneficence looking over the roads, for blind corner passing was the rule, and was accomplished with a triumphant and strident blaring of the horn that defied fate to interfere with this carefree licence to drive on the wrong side of the road. From my seat in the bus high above the road I watched, fascinated, expecting each moment to see the most horrible head-on collision, and to hear the agony of metal being twisted, torn, and crushed that I had so frequently heard in crashes on board aircraft carriers. But nothing happened. We wound our way up the long hill at the head of an impatient queue, for once awed into obeying the rules of self-preservation, and at the top turned off to take the steep, winding descent into Santa Margareta. The bus emptied there and waited for a few minutes, and I just had time to stretch my legs before we were off again, this time following the level but very narrow road that led round the coast to Portofino.

On one occasion with the intuition these drivers seem

to possess we stopped in one of the few stretches of the road where two buses could pass, and sure enough about fifteen seconds later another monster came charging round the corner, its horn braying and the echoes bouncing from the rock wall from which the road had been hewn, terrifying in its determination, its roof within inches of the rock face. The driver, with a cheerful wave of his hand, looking anywhere but at the road, gave a final toot on his horn and we were safe. But in our bus no one had noticed; two old women in earnest conversation continued their gesticulations, a young couple at the back, heads close together, were looking dreamily out to sea; the remainder looked like locals either returning to Portofino or going there for the day from Santa Margareta; they all knew each other and were shouting the commonplaces of the day as though not only the whole bus but all Italy should share them.

Presently we turned the last corner and drove into Portofino. The street in which we stopped is wide enough for a square, and here the solid necessities are offered unadorned by the tourist attractions that are the characteristic of every Riviera village, the banks, administrative buildings, plain provision shops, hardware stores, etc. The street sloped gently down to the harbour and at the bottom narrowed into a passage free from cars, where the full pressure of the tourist trade was already turned on, although it was only the end of April. There were stalls selling postcards, and stalls selling lace. Further down, shops with luxurious looking cakes and confectionery, exotic straw hats, paintings and carvings, gay shirts and shorts, pants for the girls, and all the necessities for enjoying a simple holiday! There were garlands of nuts strung together alternately, walnuts and hazelnuts, or brazilnuts and peanuts, or in a long string so that you could buy a metre. All these temptations I managed to resist, mostly because I had only enough money for a good lunch and a bottle of wine, and I didn't want to have to fit my meal to the reduced contents of my pocket. The place must live on its tourist trade, for there was little else apart from some fishing and the few yachts that accepted the shelter of the harbour for the winter. But it was obviously prospering; the new buildings going up on either side of the wide street were the signs that everywhere turned attractive simple villages into sophisticated businesses thrusting simplicity at you with such vigour that its charm was lost.

The passage led into the wide cobbled area surrounding the harbour, and this was quite unspoilt. It was surrounded by high ground except for its comparatively narrow entrance and would offer excellent shelter from all winds. There were a great many small boats, some drawn up on the cobbles and being repaired, others filling the space that was not taken up by the few yachts, some quite large, that were moored with gangplanks over the stern to the shore. I wandered along the path that led round the harbour examining the restaurants and stopping to watch a party that was in progress on board one of the larger yachts. There were a number of young people, some of them English, dressed in sweaters and brightly coloured pants, shouting, laughing and waving bottles of champagne about. As it was, they disturbed the peace of the place, because they were the only voices to be heard; but Portofino today was dead; I felt it should be throbbing with life and activity, and the party on the yacht was an earnest that it was not always like this. It was nearly one o'clock, but it had the appearance of a village not yet awake.

It was difficult to decide where to have lunch. All the restaurants looked much alike with tables and chairs outside inviting the few people who, like me, were wandering about rather aimlessly. The sun was shining, but there was little warmth in it, and the suspicion of a cold wind would make itself felt as soon as one sat down. But it was a shame to leave the sun and the colours and the quiet scene for what would probably be the very 'arty' interior of a restaurant. I ordered a St. Raphael and sat down at one of the tables in the sun. It was really a perfect day for a brisk walk, but that was not possible here; the high ground did not look very inviting, and I wondered what people who stayed here would do, apart from eating, drinking and taking motor-boat trips. There was no place for a quiet evening stroll except along the hazardous coast road by which we had come. I finished my drink; it was too cold to linger over it, and went over to a little restaurant in the corner that I liked the look of. The choice turned out to be a good one: it was bright and comfortable inside and didn't have the appearance of trying to squeeze as many people in as possible. There were amusing strips of carving on the walls that depicted lively scenes in the form of the strip cartoon. There were also some particularly lovely photographs that I would look at before going out.

I ordered some Antinori, which is my choice of Chianti whenever I can get it, and studied the menu. Presently the padrone came along and advised me. He must have thought I looked hungry and I was loth to disillusion him, particularly as there were only two other tables occupied, but he finally accepted with good grace my insistence that I did not want a four-course lunch. I sat back to enjoy the Chianti with some of those long sticks of crisp bread. Although the room was just pleasantly warm, the sun pouring on me through the closed window was deceptively hot and I felt luxuriously relaxed and in harmony with my surroundings.

My visit to Rangoon was already taking on the un-reality of a vivid dream. There had been so much bustle and activity since I returned, and now a whole world had been left behind. As so often happens in the Navy, when one job is finished and the next not yet known, one has the sense of leaving one existence and facing a new one full of unknowns. Friends and acquaintances of my two and a half years in Singapore were now pigeonholed in a clearly defined section of my past. Most of them I would never see again, and some I would run into in circumstances so widely different from those in which I knew them, that I would at first be unable to place them, and then find that I could not bring them out of their background and integrate them into the new one. But a few had been strong enough associations to carry their background with them, and with those I could take up where I left off. It is so seldom that this is so. One must generally expect each time on meeting a friend after a long period of separation to have to start the friendship again from the beginning. Two people who are not in frequent contact can so quickly grow in opposite directions, particularly when they are young, and to expect always to be able to continue a friendship where it left off is asking to be disillusioned. It might be that the period of catching up— of bridging the gap—will be very short, and in exceptional cases it can happen instantaneously. But this is rare, and it is far better not to make any assumptions but to start from the beginning and build the friendship anew. It was sad to think that I should inevitably lose so many of the good friends I had made, of all races and nationalities, and in this case the break was to be bigger than before, for there would be no more jobs. I was leaving the Navy after wearing the uniform for thirty-eight years, not to retire into comfortable inactivity—that is impossible in these days—but to find some new employment. It would mean changing the service of the Queen for that of some business executive, and entering an atmosphere where efficiency is necessarily tied to costs. There would be a whole new world of loyalties and significances to embrace, in which I should be on a very different footing with my fellow men from that to which I had become accustomed. This would not worry me, because I had never felt that any particular environment was necessary to my happiness, but the adjustment might puzzle me. I wondered whether I should find help in this from my recent practices.

I had set out to find something with which to counter the tensions of our daily life. But the full significance of what I had experienced would not be clear to me for some time. The process of adjustment to new ideas, of the absorption by the subconscious of whatever I had intuitively accepted, the gradual changing of not only habits of mind but natural mental reactions; all these things and the decisions that would spring from them should not be forced or hurried. They would come to fruition in their own time. I had been trained and become accustomed to making decisions, almost to progress from moment to moment by judging the situation and deciding the next move. It had become such a habit that I felt I was shirking responsibility if I had some important information and yet based no decision on it! Now I realized that there were many occasions when one should not *make* decisions, but instead wait patiently until the right answer comes to the surface of its own accord. In fact in all important personal decisions a period should be allowed for the rational summing up to be influenced by the deeper intuition. In the case of my experiment in mindfulness, I did not know whether there would indeed be any decisions to be expected, but there had been a great deal of new thought assimilated, and that must in time result in some change in outlook.

Had anything come to the surface yet? Had the experience brought previously gestating thoughts to maturity? I tried to review what I had learnt and to see whether any certainty had yet emerged about things that had before been uncertain. In its striking refusal to accept reliance on any outside source, from God, saints, or personalities of any kind, from ritual, formal worship, or prayer, the Buddhist training in mindfulness is in the first place a ruthless stripper of conventional religious supports. If one had the time before undertaking the discipline to stop and think, it would be a fearsome prospect to face living without the comforts with which religion surrounds us. These have their proper function, to support us while we grow the roots with which to support ourselves; but unfortunately the props, like many temporary things, become permanent through habit, and to remove them leaves us uncomfortably balanced between fear and freedom.

I had always felt, from a young man in my late teens when I first started to read Hindu philosophy, that there was a distinct dichotomy in the path to spiritual maturity. First, as in Christianity, there was a total negation of self-power, and a looking outside for help and guidance, and however much the outside source may be supposed to act through the individual the appeal was to something not already inherently possessed; a search to 'otherness' by which the self was to be transformed. In apparent opposition to this is the method of the East which requires an intense looking inward to discover the source of power and enlightenment that lies within, and a negation of only the false self leading to the unfolding of the real 'self' united in oneness with all creation. These two views were incompatible, and while each seemed to me to be convincing in its own way, it was impossible to progress without making a choice. For years this 'either-or' which had dominated my thoughts about the deepest practices of the world's religions had been demanding resolution.

And now suddenly it was no more a problem. This flash of insight occurred at a moment when I had just put my glass of wine down in a patch of sunlight that fell on the table. The sensation that accompanied it was so remarkable that it remains fresh in my memory and has now become a partner to the solution that for so long evaded me. The deep red of the wine came to me also in a flash that was quite startling in its beauty. It completely engulfed me and invaded all my senses. It was a moment of pure breath-taking, absorbing extasy. It was terribly exciting and deeply satisfying. The colour that saturated my being was very much a living power and I was emptying my heart in gratitude and at the same time tense with fear that it might leave me.

I have no idea how long I sat staring at the wine, but all at once with an immense sense of loss I saw it again as a glass of wine throwing circles of red light on the table-cloth, and although there had been nothing in my mind during this moment but colour—this deep red, the shade of which I shall never forget—immediately afterwards I realized that I now held the solution to the 'either-or' I had for so long been unable to understand. It had been in no sense worked out, but I knew that there was no longer any difficulty in understanding the two approaches, so different in conception and each so misunderstood by the other. The certainty came, not while I was thinking about it, and certainly not as the result of any previous conscious enquiry. I just suddenly knew that I had only to sort out the thoughts that were there to be picked up and examined at leisure, and this dichotomy would have been dissipated. This was an unexpected bonus from a period of strenuous attempts not to solve any abstract problems, but it had nothing to do with what I was looking for.

Was I any nearer to finding an antidote to the tensions we constantly built up in ourselves, that was a practicable one to adopt in a busy life? Almost any practice that was unusual and obvious would inevitably result in accusations of eccentricity and would have no general appeal. Without yet having had much opportunity of putting it into practice in everyday life, it seemed to me that if one were to take up Satipatthana as a regular means of detensioning one's whole body and mind and restoring their natural resistances and reactions to harmful influences, there were two types of deliberate practices that must become habits. First, a period alone each morning in the quiet of one's room or in a special room set aside for the purpose where one will not be disturbed, for the important 'rising-falling' exercise. It is in this exercise that the maximum quietening of the bodily and mental processes occurs, and where, if regularly practised, the upflowing of intuition will take place. At first half an hour at least should be set aside each morning, because the beginner will have much trouble in inducing his mind to follow the rising-falling movement for more than a few seconds at a time. The length of the period depends on how quickly the practiser can stop his mind wandering from the subject, and when fairly proficient it can be reduced to fifteen minutes. A shorter period than this is really not much use. I personally would have judged half an hour to be about the minimum, but on one occasion when I was having an interview with Shwesedi, he said it would be helpful if we did a period of meditation together, and this happened to be fifteen minutes. We were sitting on the hard floor of the lecture hall which I found so uncomfortable and therefore too distracting for effective practice, and I didn't relish the prospect of sitting there for half an hour or more struggling to ignore the powerful messages from my ankle-bones! But Shwesedi suddenly came out of it after fifteen minutes and said that was quite enough once the ability to get settled in concentration had been acquired.

There is no general rule for the time one can usefully remain in contemplation of this sort. It depends on so many things. To begin with, the time one feels is available without making the morning's routine difficult; how long it is possible to sit in a stable and upright position; the degree of concentration that has been reached; and finally but most important the beginning of the disturbing noises that the morning always brings, either in the house, or the traffic outside. In a city these are particularly disturbing because they are loud and discontinuous. The best that can be done is to select a room where they are as muffled as possible and to shut the window. It is helpful to lock the door as even the chance of someone walking in will prevent concentration, and as complete a sense of privacy as possible is essential. Much useful advice has been given in the many books that deal with meditation in detail and there is no need for me to enlarge on that here. Such things as the condition of the body, whether to wash first, the position to adopt, clothes to wear, etc., have all been fully dealt with in excellent books by both men and women with a very great experience of such disciplines, and this particular aspect of the Satipatthana training is no different from the other schools of meditation, except perhaps in the simplicity of the subject of meditation and the plain, easily understood object of the training.

The second type of exercise is of the greatest value in bringing the mind to a state of relaxed quietude at any odd moment of the day or night, when it would probably otherwise be occupied with completely idle wandering, or unnecessary and unwanted thoughts. Very often these thoughts are of anxiety, anger, wishful thinking, disappointment, regret, etc., all of which have harmful effects on the nervous and glandular balance of the body. We can deal with the tensions we must face if we employ the times when no tension need be present as recuperative interludes. This is where the real exercise of mindfulness comes in, for the mind can be withdrawn from its idle and worrying occupation and focussed, as in the Satipatthana training, either on the 'sitting-touching' contacts, or on the feet if walking in a suitable environment (but this is difficult, because the walking with contemplation must necessarily be slower, more deliberate and somewhat out of place in a busy town, except perhaps when waiting for a train!) or any of the actions of the body can be followed temporarily. Finally one can on so many occasions sit quietly relaxed, and turn one's attention to the 'rising-falling' movement without anyone else being aware that you are doing anything out of the ordinary! Making a habit of employing such moments in conscious relaxation of this sort will gradually result in the mind naturally giving up the old habit of using these periods for harping on the troubles and annoyances of daily life. It is always easier to get rid of a bad habit by cultivating a good one, and in this case it will soon become strikingly apparent that the mind prefers the relaxed contemplative state to the other; and it will draw into this state the sense impressions that can and should be a constant source of satisfaction, enjoyment and appreciation of beauty, but which we seldom allow ourselves time for conscious attention.

The secret of counteracting the destructive poisons of tension is not then what so many people expect and hope to find, a pill to be swallowed, or even some exercise to be given a few minutes' attention each day. It is in the end a completely changed outlook, brought about it is true by exercise, but resulting in something that is a continuous refreshment, and not a shot in the arm administered from time to time. Such a new outlook and its effect is not something that can be won in a few days, but from the moment one starts progress begins, and every little attempt to bar the poisons with the most effective and powerful weapon at our disposal, our minds, has a double result. It prevents the harmful effects that an untidy and troubled mind bring to the body, and it allows the natural and very strong recuperative powers of the mind to influence the whole body.

If meditative habits like this could be developed, there was no doubt in my mind that they would have the integrating effect I had been searching for, and they would not necessitate the adoption of any eccentricities. There was no room for doubt because I had experienced the full effect of the emptying of the mind of all unwanted activity; moreover I had had a glimpse of the immense power that was revealed by the process of collecting in all wasteful effort and learning to concentrate. This was perhaps the most exciting immediate discovery, the fact that it was possible with comparatively little effort to take complete control of the mind, and to set oneself on the path, not only of using its full capacity, but of obtaining through it insight of new knowledge and the awareness of new fields of experience.

My meal had come and gone; I forget what it was, but the wine was delicious and fully lived up to its aristocratic colour. The sun had been obscured by low scudding clouds, and a few local women were hurrying across the cobbles that surrounded the harbour, hugging their shawls round their shoulders against the cold wind, in haste to avoid the rain that was certainly coming. I had a few minutes more before I must leave to catch my bus back to Genoa. There would be little chance, once I was back on board, for further contemplative studies. The last few days of the voyage would be full of social activities that would be difficult to avoid: the voyage so far had been long enough for most of the passengers to get to know one another. There had been at first small groups of acquaintances and these had gradually grown as the shuffleboard and other deck games got under way; the bridge and poker parties followed rather later. But on the whole, except in the bar, the foreigners (for it was a foreign ship) had respected the traditional British reserve that the majority of the passengers displayed. But this was now beginning to melt, and would soon be followed by the address-taking and promises that precede the final disembarking.

I did not particularly want in any case to sit alone and pursue my thoughts, for I still knew that more time would be required for the process of digestion and assimilation.

Here in the mellow warmth of the sun and with the prospect of a good meal and a bottle of wine it was easy to fall into a relaxed and contemplative mood. The real test was whether I should be able to recall this mood at will, and that test must lie ahead. I should find out whether what I had learnt would remain with me as a source of mental and physical refreshment, always at hand; or whether it would be like so many of the courses I had done—a flash in the pan that made one an expert for a short while, a pseudo-expert for somewhat longer, ending up with becoming a 'one-time' expert or one who has forgotten all about the subject! I did not think it would be like this because it had bitten deeper than the sort of superficial information one absorbed in technical courses. But it would have to be kept alive, of that I was sure. In the difficult days that were to come, in all the domestic and other complications of a new existence, I should have to find time to keep the technique going.

I paid my bill and got up to go, but wandered first over to the photograph hanging at the end of the room. It was of a ship alongside the docks and was taken from just ahead of the bow on the jetty. There was a small boy standing by an old wooden bollard that carried the bow line, and this hemp line was the central subject of the picture leading up to the ship well above. It was a simple but extremely effective composition and the inference was clear. The boy's entranced gaze followed up the hemp line to the great ship where his ambition lay, and where he stood the focus was sharp, but it tailed off to where the details were blurred and indistinct as the line passed through the fairlead on to the forecastle. It was obviously an enlargement, and the picture itself was some twelve by twenty-four inches. As I stood and looked at it the rain came down and I hurried out, turning up the collar of my thin coat. The path leading up to the bus park was now a small river, and I felt tempted to join the few tourists sheltering in the doorways of the shops. But I was still near enough to Naval discipline to be conscious of getting back on time, and I splashed my way determinedly past the stalls, hurriedly covered with tarpaulins, back to my bus.

It had been a pleasant and useful interlude. I had come to the satisfactory conclusion that I need make no decisions: things would work themselves out; if the seed that had been sown was fertile it would germinate in good time. Let it do this unharassed, unpressed; meanwhile all the contacts that life would bring from the now familiar ship to the unknown and unplanned track that lay ahead, would in one way or another mould the new knowledge of myself that I had found into harmony with the life I must live. For that is the purpose of life—to be lived, not to be escaped from: that it should be the test and arbiter of theories and discoveries and knowledge. The false would not lead to happiness and a fuller life, but to narrower and restricted experience. The true would in time be clear with strength and certainty. Given the patience to wait, and the discernment to interpret, this, in spite of all the appearances to the contrary, I believe.